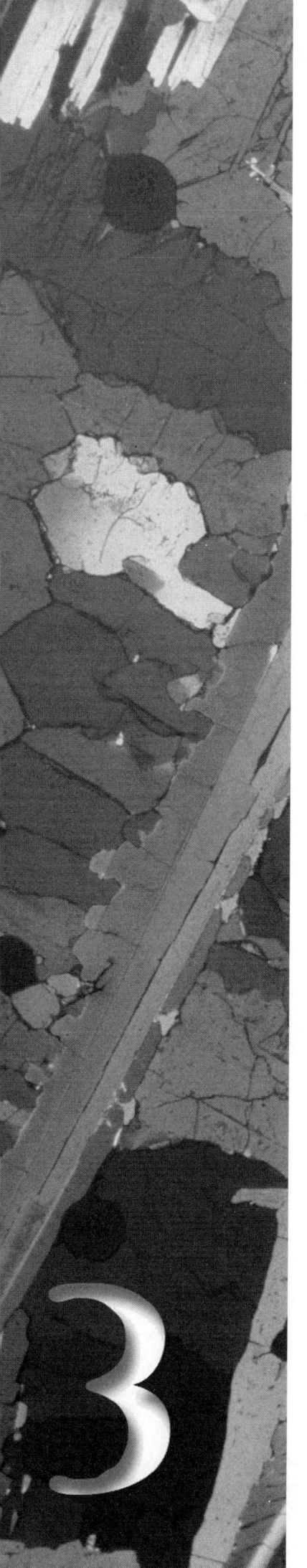

English Frameworking
Teacher's Resources

Contents

	Page no. Teacher's notes	Worksheets
Objectives matching grid	3	
Introduction	4	
Reviewing Year 8	6	41
Imagine, explore, entertain	9	51
Inform, explain, describe	15	76
Persuade, argue, advise	20	98
Analyse, review, comment	24	120
Plan, draft, present	30	141
Preparing for NCTs	36	160

Long-term, medium-term and short-term teaching plans are available on the accompanying CD-ROM in the form of customizable files that can be adapted to create a scheme of work.

Julia Strong
Deputy Director, National Literacy Trust
Pam Bloomfield
Kim Richardson

National Literacy Trust

Published by HarperCollins*Publishers* Limited
77–85 Fulham Palace Road
Hammersmith
London W6 8JB

www.**Collins**Education.com
On-line support for schools and colleges

© 2002 Julia Strong, Pam Bloomfield and Kim Richardson
First published 2002

ISBN 0 00 711354 4

Julia Strong, Pam Bloomfield and Kim Richardson assert their moral rights to be identified as the authors of this work.

All rights reserved. Any educational institution that has purchased one copy of this publication may make duplicate copies for use exclusively within that institution. Permission does not extend to reproduction, storage in a retrieval system, or transmittal in any form or by any means, electronic, mechanical, photocopying, recording or otherwise, of duplicate copies for loaning, renting or selling to any other institution without the publisher's prior consent.

British Library Cataloguing in Publication Data
A catalogue record for this publication is available from the British Library.

Acknowledgements
The publishers gratefully acknowledge the following for permission to reproduce copyright material. Every effort has been made to trace copyright holders, but in some cases this has proved impossible. The publishers would be happy to hear from any copyright holder that has not been acknowledged.

Text: Extract from *The Poisonwood Bible* by Barbara Kingsolver, published by Faber and Faber in 1999. Reprinted by permission of the publishers and the author's agent David Grossman Literary Agency, London (p44). Extract from *Design and Technology Food Foundation Course* by Sue Plews, Janet Inglis and Eileen Chapman, published by Collins Educational 1999. Reprinted by permission of the publisher (p44). Extract from *Strength to Love* by Martin Luther King, published by Hodder & Stoughton Limited. Reprinted by permission of Laurence Pollinger Limited and the Estate of Martin Luther King (p44). Extract from *Never Again: Britain 1945-1951* by Peter Hennessey, published by Jonathan Cape 1992. Reprinted by permission of Sheil Land Associates Limited (p45). Extract from *The Times Atlas of World History*, 4th edition by Geoffrey Parker, published by HarperCollins 1993. Reprinted by permission of the publishers (p45). Extract from *Nukespeak: The Media and the Bomb* by John Pilger, published by Comedia Publishing Group. Reprinted by permission of the publishers (p44). Extract from *Your Life 1* by John Foster, published by Collins Educational 2000. Reprinted by permission of the publishers (p45). Extract from 'This Fella I Knew' from *Walking the Dog* by Bernard MacLaverty, published by Jonathan Cape. © Bernard MacLaverty 1994. Reprinted by permission of Rogers, Coleridge & White Limited, 20 Powis Mews, London W11 1JN. All rights reserved (p51). Extract from 'A Woman of No Standing' by Brendan Behan from *After the Wake* published by The O'Brien Press Limited. Copyright © Brendan Behan, reprinted by permission of the publishers (p54). 'Stench of Kerosene' by Amrita Pritam, translated from the Punjabi by Khushwant Singh. Reprinted by permission of Khushwant Singh, India (pp55-7). Extract from *In Love and Trouble* by Alice Walker published by The Women's Press. Reprinted by permission of David Higham Associates Limited (pp60-61). Extract from *Transylvania and Beyond* by Dervla Murphy, published by John Murray 1992. Reprinted by permission of the publishers (pp67-8). Extract from *Notes from a Small Island* by Bill Bryson, published by Transworld Publishers, a division of The Random House Group Limited. © Bill Bryson. All rights reserved. Reprinted with permission (p72). Extracts from *The Alexander Shakespeare: Macbeth*, 2nd edition, published by HarperCollins. Reprinted by permission of the publishers (pp81, 83, 85-6). 'Melt Down' by Paul Brown, from *The Guardian*, 18 July 2001. Reprinted by permission of The Guardian (p91). Extract from www.epa.gov. Reprinted with permission (p93). Extract from www.highnorth.no. Reprinted with permission (p95). Extract from www.crin.org. Reprinted with permission (p96). Extract from *Amusing Ourselves to Death* by Neil Postman, published by Methuen 1987. Reprinted by permission of Methuen Publishing Limited (p110). Extracts from www.labour.org.uk. Reprinted by permission of the Labour Party (pp111, 116). Extracts from www.conservatives.com. Reprinted by permission of the Conservative Party (pp111, 115). Extracts from www.libdems.org.uk. Reprinted by permission of the Liberal Democrats (pp112, 117). Extract from *The Week* 'Election briefing: How the parties differ over … crime', 2 June 2001. Reprinted by permission of The Week (p114). Letter to the editor, *The Independent*, 29 May 2001 (p119). Extracts from *Pygmalion* by George Bernard Shaw, © The Public Trustee as Executor of the Estate of George Bernard Shaw 1957. Reprinted by permission of the Society of Authors on behalf of the Bernard Shaw Estate (pp120-21). Extract from *Our Day Out* by Willy Russell, published by Heinemann Educational. © 1976 W. R. Ltd. Reprinted by permission of Casarotto Ramsay & Associates Limited (pp126-7). Extract from *The Big Issue (South West)*, no. 453 (3-9 Sept 2001) © The Big Issue, South West. Reprinted with permission (p132). Review of *My Fair Lady* by Nicholas de Jongh, slightly abridged from *The Evening Standard*, 16 March 2001. Reprinted by permission of Atlantic Syndication (p134). Extract from Tony Parson's interview with Victoria Beckham, from *The Mirror*, 14 September 2001. Reprinted by permission of The Mirror (p135). Extract 'The Panel: The new Penguin English Dictionary contains a lexicon of teenage slang. Will this damage their use of 'proper' English?' From *The Guardian*, 8 August 2001. Copyright © The Guardian, 8 August 2001. Reprinted with permission (p140). 'Strugnell's Sonnets IV' by Wendy Cope from *Making Cocoa for Kingsley Amis* published by Faber and Faber Limited 1997. Reprinted by permission of the publishers (p142). 'Anyone lived in a pretty how town' by E. E. Cummings, from *Collected Poems* published by W. W. Norton, USA (p146). 'Musée des Beaux Arts' by W. H. Auden, from *Collected Poems* by W. H. Auden, published by Faber and Faber Limited. Copyright © 1940 by W. H. Auden. Reprinted by permission of Curtis Brown Limited, New York (p148). 'Not My Best Side' by U. A. Fanthorpe from *Side Effects* published by Peterloo Poets, 1978. Reprinted by permission of the author (p149). 'I Would Like to Be a Dot in a Painting by Miró' by Moniza Alvi, from *Carrying My Wife* published by Bloodaxe Books 2000. Reprinted by permission of the publishers (p150). 'In Mrs Tilscher's Class' by Carol Ann Duffy from *The Other Country* published by Anvil Press Poetry in 1990. Reprinted by permission of Anvil Press Poetry Limited (p153). 'Flat-track Family' by Dan Joyce, slightly abridged from *The Guardian*, 4 August 2001 © Dan Joyce. Reprinted by permission of The Guardian (pp163-4).

Photos: High North Alliance (p95); Child Rights Information Network (p96); PA Photos (p116).

Internal artwork by Andrew Quelch (pp51, 57, 63); Jennifer Ward (pp68, 137); Steve Smith (p105).

Cover and internal design by Ken Vail Graphic Design, Cambridge
Commissioned by Helen Clark
Edited by Kim Richardson and Angela Wigmore
Picture research by Gavin Jones
Medium-term and short-term plans (CD-ROM) by Antonia Sharpe
Production by Katie Morris
Printed and bound by Martins

You might also like to visit
www.**fire**and**water**.co.uk
The book lover's website

NLT website
www.literacytrust.org.uk

Objectives matching grid

This grid indicates where each of the English framework objectives has been targeted in the Student's Book. Key objectives are in bold.

Word		Sentence		Text				Speaking and listening	
				Reading		Writing			
Objectives	Page nos	Objectives	Page nos	Objectives	Page nos	Objectives	Page nos	Objectives	Page nos
1	30–31	**1**	14–15	**1**	54–5, 148–9	**1**	8–9, 14–15, 122–3, 148-9	**1**	12–13, 112–13, 126–7
2	10–11	**2**	98–9	**2**	58–9	**2**	112–13, 120–21, 126–7	**2**	18–25
3	10–11, 26–7, 34–5, 58–9, 136–9	**3**	78–9, 82–3, 96–101, 110–11	3	12–13, 100–01	**3**	14–15, 120–23, 132–43	3	80–81, 100–01
4	34–5, 58–9, 134–7	4	34–5, 78–9, 100–01, 104–5, 122–3	4	52–5	4	56–61, 82–3, 114–15, 118–19, 124–5	4	12–13, 112–13, 126–7
5	20–21, 28–9	5	78–9, 102–5, 122–3	5	148–9	**5**	26–7	5	76–7
6	8–9, 96–7, 114–15	**6**	74–7	6	18–25	6	36–7	6	76–7
7	22–5	7	8–9, 44–5, 82–3	7	74–5, 98–9, 116–23	7	36–7, 132–5	7	74–7
8	74–7	8	52–3, 56–61	8	56–7	8	108–15	8	112–13, 126–7
		9	78–9, 98–9, 104–5, 122–3	9	32–5	**9**	50–51, 59–61, 104–5	**9**	74–7
		10	86–7, 90–91, 104–5	10	70–71	10	50–51, 102–5	10	10–11, 124–7
		11	42–3, 48–9, 54–5	11	22–5, 28–33	11	36–7, 48–9, 136–7	11	94–5
				12	64–5, 74–5, 78–9	12	58–61, 82–3	12	88–93
				13	6–7, 146–9	13	78–9, 82–3, 138–9	**13**	46–7, 88–9
				14	40–41, 44–51, 86–91, 140–43	**14**	78–9	14	92–5
				15	42–3, 48–51, 64–9, 72–3	15	70–71, 80–83	15	94–9
				16	18–21	**16**	104–5		
				17	108–9, 116–23	17	34–5, 88–9		
				18	22–5				

English Frameworking 3: Teacher's Resources © HarperCollins*Publishers* 2002

Teacher's notes

Introduction

This is the third and final book of the *English Frameworking* series. It has been designed to build on what the students have learnt in the earlier two books to help them become powerful communicators. It provides both thorough preparation for the Year 9 National Curriculum Tests and a sound foundation for GCSE work.

The editors were aware of the danger that working to the framework might result in fragmented practice; *English Frameworking* has therefore been devised in coherent sections that deliver one or two broad aims, as well as delivering all the objectives of the English framework.

English Frameworking:

- builds on the interactive approaches of the literacy hour providing progression from Key Stage 2 without overlap
- is set in contexts that students should find enjoyable, motivating and challenging
- meets the requirements of the national curriculum
- delivers all the English framework objectives
- is organized into coherent sections guided by key broad aims based on the framework
- offers flexibility – you can dip into the course or follow it through
- takes the paperwork out of planning: starter sessions and lesson plans are included; short-, medium- and long-term plans are available on the CD-ROM
- is assessment focused – formative assessment, review and target setting is built into the structure of the sections, while a section on NCTs helps prepare students for the assessment of formal exams
- integrates the six non-fiction text types plus narrative that underpin the national literacy strategy into the fiction and non-fiction text triplets of the national curriculum
- offers a mainstream course supporting students working at national curriculum levels 3–5 with suggestions within the teacher's notes for further differentiation
- has been trialled with students, teachers and advisory teachers both in and out of the pilot areas
- helps integrate literacy across the curriculum into whole-school practice
- encourages students to see how their literacy skills can be extended right across the curriculum.

The art of effective teaching is the formative assessment that enables any teacher to plan effectively, putting in the steps that will build on the students' existing knowledge. No textbook can replace that expertise. However, *English Frameworking* has been designed to help teachers intervene effectively. Its structure is underpinned by the need for formative assessment.

Refer to the introduction to the Teacher's Resources of Book 1 of this series for information and guidance on the following:

- Assessment and target setting
- Spelling and spelling logs
- Cross-curricular framework objectives (see also update on page 5 below)
- Extended writing
- Supporting writing and the equipment that helps you do the job
- Reading records and extended reading
- Differentiation.

For notes on the lesson structure, see the introduction to the Teacher's Resources to Book 2 of the series.

Adapting the sections to meet the needs of your class

English Frameworking offers teachers an imaginative series of sections that cover all the national requirements, plus the space to adapt these sections to meet the needs of particular classes. No two classes are alike and all general planning needs to be adapted in the light of students' needs.
Each book contains 65 teaching sessions of approximately one hour. The average teaching time per year for English in Key Stage 3 is 114 hours. Thus *English Frameworking* allows space for teachers to go at a slower pace to meet the needs of their class, as well as providing opportunities for teachers to build in additional work alongside the programme to encourage extended reading and writing. These Teacher's Resources include suggestions for how this could be done.

In particular the Teacher's Resources flag up opportunities for developing:

- Spelling logs
- Literacy across the curriculum
- Extended writing
- Reading records and extended reading
- Differentiation.

Teacher's notes

Literacy across the curriculum and the cross-curricular objectives

By this time, your school will probably have selected its cross-curricular literacy objectives. The NLS is advising schools to use the English framework objectives to guide the development of literacy across the curriculum with particular emphasis on the highlighted objectives – those English objectives that are seen as more significant and thus need to be revisited throughout the year to ensure full coverage. This, of course, is to assume that the objectives for teaching English and the objectives for delivering literacy across the curriculum are one and the same, which many would argue is not the case.

Sensibly, the NLS is recommending that 'schools focus their energies on a small and memorable number of cross-curricular literacy priorities in each year'. The four objectives below have been suggested by the NLS for Year 9, but schools are encouraged to select their own objectives from the framework in the light of local need.

1. Compare and use different ways of opening, developing, linking and completing paragraphs.

2. Synthesize information from a range of sources, shaping material to meet the reader's needs.

3. Write with differing degrees of formality, relating vocabulary and grammar to context, e.g. using the active or passive voice.

4. Discuss and evaluate conflicting evidence to arrive at a considered viewpoint.

These objectives, however, are worded with the students as the audience in mind. Moreover, they have been written from the perspective of the English curriculum. Schools may find it helpful to reword their selected objectives with their immediate audience in mind – teachers from all subject areas – for example:

1. **Paragraphing**: Help students develop their ability to write as appropriate to your subject using appropriate ways of opening, developing, linking and completing paragraphs.

2. **Writing**: Help students synthesize information from a range of sources, bearing in mind the audience they are writing for and shaping material to meet the reader's needs.

3. **Writing**: Think about what degree of formality of writing is appropriate to your subject. Help students write with the appropriate degree of formality given the nature of particular writing tasks, relating vocabulary and grammar to context, e.g. using the active or passive voice.

4. **Speaking, listening and thinking**: Help students to discuss and evaluate conflicting evidence to arrive at a considered viewpoint.

Alternative versions of the proposed Year 7 and Year 8 objectives are available on www.literacytrust.org.uk/database/secondary/objectives.html

Adapting English Frameworking

Feedback from Books 1 and 2 has resulted in the following two frequently asked questions.

What's the best way to adapt English Frameworking to 50-minute lessons?

One possible solution to the problem of the 50-minute lesson is to remove the stand-alone starters from any lessons where these exist, thus making the remaining material more manageable within a shorter lesson. Then select those lessons that, given the nature of the material and your class, could well be extended over two lessons. (There are fewer than 70 spreads in each *English Frameworking* book, whereas there are probably at least 120 English lessons in a year.) Add the stand-alone starters to these additional lessons.

What's the best way to adapt English Frameworking to suit lower-ability groups?

Many teachers have found the material in *English Frameworking* successful with lower-ability groups but often more time is needed to help students work effectively. Many teachers have doubled the amount of time spent on some of the activities to allow more time for modelling for students how to do the work and for supporting their work. As pointed out above, there are nearly twice as many English lessons in the year as outlined lessons in *English Frameworking*. This allows time for such an approach, as well as for developing extended reading.

Teacher's notes

Reviewing Year 8 and looking forward to Year 9

Introduction

The first section in *English Frameworking 3* is introductory and focuses on strengthening a range of key skills. In the first lesson each student analyses not just their skills as a reader but their attitude to reading. It sets the tone by attempting to help students appreciate how valuable a skill reading is – one that needs nurturing. This provides the foundation for an ongoing evaluation of reading skills and preferences which is built on throughout the year and consolidated in the final section.

The text analysis work in the second lesson helps to strengthen students' confidence in analysing text types using the appropriate vocabulary. It also provides space to reflect on their writing skills. This is consolidated by the writing task in the final lesson of this section.

The third lesson focuses on students' ability to think creatively about ways of improving spelling in all areas of the curriculum. A series of spelling activities throughout the book gradually builds up their ability to select appropriate spelling strategies to overcome persistent problems.

Lesson four provides a useful way of improving students' speaking and listening skills through playing the game Alibis – an activity that students find very engaging. This leads to a challenging writing task in the final lesson which helps develop the students' ability to construct effective formal essays. This skill is revisited throughout the book to provide a firm foundation for the formal writing demands of GCSE.

To read is to soar

Objectives targeted TR13
Starter

Begin the starter by selling reading along the lines suggested. The Cuban tobacco workers' story is included to encourage students to recognize why they should value and develop their reading skills. Tell the story of the Cuban tobacco workers in the 19th century and read the law that was brought in to try to stop the workforce from becoming literate.

Introduction

Give every student a copy of **Worksheet 1** to help them analyse the range of their reading. Refer them to their reading journals so that their analysis can be based on what they have actually read.

Divide the class into groups with as far as possible shared reading interests and get each group to draw up its recommended reads as suggested in the Student's Book.

Development

After they have listed their key strengths and weaknesses as a reader, give every student a copy of the reading skills analysis grid (**Worksheet 2**).

Extended reading

The key purpose here is to encourage students to widen their reading by hearing from their peers about books they've enjoyed. A useful resource to strengthen this activity is the magazine *Boox*, which focuses on teenagers recommending good reads. Find out more on www.boox.org.uk

There is a wide range of suggestions for encouraging reading among secondary students on the National Literacy Trust's website – see www.literacytrust.org.uk/Campaign/Secondary.html. If possible, liaise with the school librarian to have a wide range of books available for borrowing at the end of this lesson which reflect both the categories of text covered in the introduction activity and the titles liable to be selected by the groups.

Extended writing

A useful way of extending this activity is to get students to write their own reading autobiography. Use the text on page 7 below (written by Gary, a 14-year-old student) to launch the idea and suggest they begin with the words 'I took to reading like …'. The results can be both entertaining and enlightening and provide a good springboard from which to negotiate reading programmes to extend the reading of all students.

Teacher's notes

Reading autobiography

I took to reading like a duck takes to water. I've always found it an enjoyable experience and, as I've grown older, I've read more and more.

The first books I read were Peter and Jane. I found these incredibly boring compared with the books my mum would read when I went to bed. My mum read me Mr Men books and Enid Blyton stories. My favourite stories were set in a magic faraway tree. It was a land where chocolates grew on trees and the rain came down as 'pop' which I found incredibly amusing.

I would fall asleep dreaming myself into the story and often finding my dreams more adventurous than the stories themselves. This gave me encouragement to express myself in the last year of infant school and on into junior school in the way of writing stories.

The Mr Men books were also highly sought after bedtime reading. I would struggle through reading the books with my mother egging me onwards. After reading a Mr Men book at night time, to have to read a Peter and Jane book the next day seemed a completely worthless experience. I would speed through these books with the greatest of ease but because, in my haste to get through the reading matter in front of me, I would make an occasional error, my teacher mistook this for lack of ability and would say:

'Now, Gary, that isn't how it goes, is it?'
'I know,' I would try to tell her.
But she would carry on: 'Now say it slowly.'
'Yeaaaaaaaaaas, Miss, "Peter threw the ball at the window."'
'Well done! See, you can do it if you try.'

I couldn't believe my teacher could be so naïve, no, even stupid, in believing I couldn't read 'window'. But still my infuriating teacher insisted on my reading yet another tedious Peter and Jane book.

The ingredients of text

Objectives targeted W6; S7; TW1
Starter

Divide the class into seven groups. Give every group a set of cards of the key terminology related to text (**Worksheet 3**) and allocate each group a different text type. Explain the categories 'Typical ingredients' and 'Not typical ingredients', so the groups are clear about the differences. For example, the term 'omniscient author' would be in the 'Typical ingredients' category if your text type was narrative, but would be in the 'Not typical ingredients' category if you had any other text type. Emphasize and explain the word 'typical' – they are looking for usual ingredients, not possible ingredients.

The 'Question mark' category is both for terms that are disputed and for terms the students may have forgotten the meaning of. This category makes it easier for the teacher to go round the groups and discuss any terms groups are having difficulties with.

The important thing to stress is the quality of the discussion that underlies the decisions that they make.

Differentiation

Groups that would find this task difficult could be allocated the easier text types. In this exercise the easier texts are narrative, instruction, recount and information. The most difficult is the discursive passage. Alternatively, the teacher could go over some of the key terms with the class, discussing which texts they most clearly relate to.

Introduction

Now give every group the text that matches the category they were allocated (**Worksheets 4a–b**) and explain what they have to do as outlined in the Student's Book. Also provide each group with an OHT of their text for them to annotate following their discussion, and remind them that each member of the group should take part in the presentation to the class of the features of their text.

Remind the class about the importance of being good listeners when other groups are presenting their text. Stress the importance of their using this feedback time to reflect on their ability to write in these different types of text in preparation for the analysis they will be completing in the next activity.

Development

Give every student a copy of **Worksheet 5** to help them analyse their writing skills and set writing targets for the coming half term.

Spelling and vocabulary across the curriculum

Objectives targeted W2, 3; SL10

This spread pulls together all the work on spelling that students should have been doing in all curriculum areas. Its central purpose is to help students transfer their spelling skills to all areas. The vocabulary

Teacher's notes

focused on should have been covered by the appropriate areas in the first two years of Key Stage 3.

Starter

Divide the class into six groups and give every group a set of the geometry-related vocabulary cards (**Worksheet 6**) consisting of 23 terms and five headings. Explain that they have to place the words under the most appropriate heading. Remind them that they may be tested on the spelling of these words at the end of the lesson.

Introduction

Having just done an activity designed to strengthen their understanding of some of the vocabulary related to triangles and angles, they now have the task of seeing if they can come up with an activity to strengthen understanding of the meaning or spelling of words related to a different area of the curriculum. Allocate each group a subject area and give them the related list of 25 words cut into the six subject area strips (**Worksheet 7**). Present the activity as a challenge. Stress that they do not have to use all or any of the words they have been allocated as long as they use words that relate to their subject area.

Development

Emphasize the importance of being a constructive listener when hearing the other groups present their ideas.

Plenary

Select 20 words from those that were worked on for the end of lesson spelling test and relate this to the homework.

The alibi challenge

Objectives targeted TR3; SL1, 4

The game Alibis is not only very popular but is excellent for building speaking and listening skills since the students have to listen very carefully and assess the significance of what they have heard in order to ask telling questions to later suspects. You may wish to extend the activity over two lessons to develop these skills further and see if any group can outwit the questioners.

Starter

Explain the game Alibis briefly to all the class and then ask for volunteers to construct the first alibi. Select volunteers from outside normal friendship groupings. Set a time limit of around three minutes for the construction of the alibi.

While the alibi group is outside the room, guide the class on how to be effective questioners along the lines suggested in the starter and the introduction. Advise the class to watch facial expression as well as listen carefully since this tends to indicate which questions the suspects were unprepared for.

Introduction

Stress the importance of noting down points to be followed up and including any significant details. Demonstrate how to draw up a weaknesses grid like the one on page 13 so that everyone keeps a running record of weaknesses. Call in the first suspect. Act as a referee calling on questioners in turn so that all can hear the questions and answers. Intervene as necessary to help the class cross-question effectively and appropriately. Remind the class to note down on their whiteboards or paper any promising questions that need following up.

Help them use some of the question approaches outlined in the Student's Book. Try to ensure as wide a spread of questioners as possible and encourage students to follow up the fruitful lines of questioning opened up by others. When you think that the class has opened up sufficient fruitful lines of questioning to be able to break the alibi when subsequent suspects are called, call in the next suspect. Allow the first suspect to remain in the room on the understanding that they face away from the class and the next suspect and make no attempt to communicate.

Help the class to focus questions appropriately so that they exploit all the weaknesses opened up by the cross-questioning of the first suspect. Follow the same procedure with the last suspect. Remind students to keep a record of significant weaknesses.

Development

Give every student a copy of **Worksheet 8** on which to record the key weaknesses in the alibi and their significance. See if the class can agree which points were the most significant and rank the points accordingly.

Then go through the whole procedure again with a second alibi group. As pointed out in the Student's Book, both suspects and questioners will have learnt from the first alibi group, so the quality of alibi and questioning should improve with each round.

Plenary

Use the plenary to tease out what the students have learnt from playing this game.

Teacher's notes

Differentiation

Try to support students who would not normally speak in whole-class situations. As useful lines of questioning come into your head, quietly feed ideas to a traditional non-speaker to help give them the confidence to intervene.

Explaining Alibis in a formal essay pg 14–15

Objectives targeted S1; TW1, **3**

Starter [ws 9]

Draw everyone's attention to the essay they will be writing this lesson.

Divide the class up into groups. Give every group a set of sentence starters (**Worksheet 9**) for them to sequence into a logical order to help structure this essay. Encourage the groups when they feed back to present their sequence as if they were teaching the class.

Introduction

The purpose of these questions is to help the class recognize the fact that many texts do not fit neatly into one text category but may have elements of several, and that the ingredients will reflect this complexity. Their own essay question, for example, demands both explanation and analysis.

Ask for a volunteer to model how to continue the introduction following the opening: 'The purpose of the game Alibis is …'. Outlaw 'The class has been playing Alibis' approach since this leads into a recount style of writing which is not required.

Development

Remind the students to look at the writing targets they set themselves earlier (**Worksheet 5**). Draw their attention to all the elements that they have in front of them to help them with their essay. The starter (once sequenced correctly) serves as a writing frame, both for structuring the essay and providing a way in for each paragraph. There is also a notice board on which are pinned useful connectives and other words and phrases. This level of support is offered because writing clearly about how to play Alibis, and then analysing the judgements that were made and what was learnt, requires significant writing skills.

Differentiation

Students who will find this task difficult should be encouraged to use the writing frame that the sequenced sentence starters provide to get them going in the right direction. The peer-group marking should help students to recognize weaknesses in their own work, which they can then rectify for homework.

Extended writing

You may wish to add in an extra lesson to provide the time to go over this piece of writing, drawing on the difficulties experienced and building in work accordingly. This could allow you time to model areas of difficulty and for guided writing.

Reviewing what's been learnt pg 16

This introductory section should have given students the opportunity to reflect on their skills as readers, writers, speakers and listeners. The reviewing section helps them set SMART targets for the first half term of the new year.

Imagine, explore, entertain

Introduction pg 17

A central focus of this section is to encourage students to think about language patterns and the origin of words as well as narrative structure. The four short stories selected have been chosen for the quality of the writing and power of each story, despite the brevity of each, and for the fact that all four give you an insight into the culture within which they were written. All are challenging. The variety of narrative structure and style that they represent should help strengthen students' understanding of these aspects of text and strengthen their ability to select their own perspective when writing a short story.

The second half of the section presents a range of different travel writing and builds up to a formal essay comparing the purpose and style of extracts from Daniel Defoe's and Bill Bryson's tours of the British Isles written four centuries apart. The range of examples is used to help build students' confidence and expertise in writing an effective traveller's tale themselves.

This section, along with the 'Plan, draft, present' section, covers all the writing objectives under 'Imagine, explore, entertain' for Year 9. As none of

Teacher's notes

the set objectives encourages extended creative writing, however, creative writing objectives have been added to maximize opportunities for students to experiment with this type of writing.

Irish storytelling (1) pg 18–19

Objectives targeted TR6, **16**; SL2

Starter [ws 10]

Give every student a copy of the opening of 'This Fella I Knew' (**Worksheet 10**) and explain that the group should mark up just one copy of the text to indicate the words or phrases that differ from the pattern of Standard English. During the feedback, introduce the concept of the oral tradition and relate it to this story. It may help to remind students where they have discussed the oral tradition before, e.g. the stories of Nasreddin Hodja, and see which students in the class have experience of the oral tradition within their culture.

Differentiation

This activity is made much easier if the teacher reads the passage to the groups before they begin.

Introduction

Introduce 'This Fella I Knew' as suggested in the Student's Book. Read the story to the class. It will work better as a story if you read from the beginning, even though the students are now familiar with the opening paragraphs. The students' ability to do the ensuing work will be greatly dependent on the quality of the reading given. Remind the students to think about the language and narrative structure of the story while they are listening.

Development [ws 11]

Give every group a copy of the analysis grid on 'This Fella I Knew' (**Worksheet 11**) which is structured to help them internalize the PECs (Point, Evidence, Comment) approach to analysing text. Remind the students of this.

Irish storytelling (2) pg 20–21

Objectives targeted W5; TR6, **16**; SL2

Starter [ws 12]

When introducing this word-origin activity, as outlined in the Student's Book, it would be useful if it could be linked to any languages spoken by students in the class. Allow opportunity for discussion of the attempt by some countries to 'conserve' their languages. For example, the Turkish equivalent of the Académie Française is the pure Turkish movement which invents words based on Turkish roots to try to stop the import of foreign words like 'computer' or 'plastic' into the language. Give every group a set of word cards (**Worksheet 12**). These words have been deliberately chosen so that not all will be known: the students will have to refer to a dictionary, so ensure that each group has a quality dictionary that includes word origins.

Introduction [ws 13]

Give every student a copy of the continuation of 'A Woman of No Standing' (**Worksheet 13**). Read the story aloud to the students: a quality reading will greatly help all students grasp the narrative approach of the story and the role of the narrator within it. Remind the students to listen to the rhythm of the speech patterns of the story, consider the narrative style and decide who the writer wants the reader to sympathize with while they are listening to it.

Development

At a first glance all the questions on 'A Woman of No Standing' look quite easy, but questions 3 and 4 are more difficult because there are no precise answers. These questions have been included to encourage students to be tentative and to express views based on deduction and overall impression. This is why the quality of the original reading of the story is crucial. Again encourage students to internalize the **Point, Evidence, Comment** approach to analysing text; here the questions are harder, to build up the students' analysis skills and confidence.

Layers of meaning pg 22–3

Objectives targeted W7; TR6, 11, 18; SL2

Starter [ws 14]

Before beginning the story you may wish to use kerosene/paraffin as a useful example of the way words develop. The word kerosene is used in most of the English-speaking world but in the UK paraffin is the more common word. Kerosene comes from the Greek word keros (wax). According to the *Oxford Library of Words and Phrases III Word Origins* the word paraffin comes from the Latin words *parum* (too little/barely) and *affinis* (related). It was given this name because of its neutral quality and

Teacher's notes

the small affinity it possesses for other bodies.

Give every student a copy of 'Stench of Kerosene' (**Worksheets 14a–c**). This story relies on implied layers of meaning; thus again a quality reading of the story by the teacher to bring out its meaning is essential to support the students in the ensuing work. Remind the class to think about the way the writer has structured the story and to note how seemingly unimportant details take on significance as the story develops.

Introduction

Give every group a set of the structure cards on 'Stench of Kerosene' (**Worksheet 15**) plus a set of the significant-points-within-the-story cards (**Worksheet 16**). Starting with the structure cards, show them how to begin to sequence their cards, pointing out that any cards that are flashbacks are shaded and should be placed in the top row. When they have completed this, remind them to place the significant-points-within-the-story cards against the appropriate moments of the story.

A set of both sets of cards in OHT form will help feedback on this.

Differentiation

This task is made easier if the cards are read to the class or the teacher works with the group that would have the most difficulty with this task.

Development

The work in the introduction activity should have prepared the class to answer the questions here. Further support could be given by encouraging students to confer briefly with a neighbour before volunteering to answer to the whole class.

Homework and extended reading

This homework should strengthen the work that students did in the first section on reflecting on their reading. Liaise with the school library to supplement the range of material that is available for students to borrow to extend their reading in this area. Where possible get students to recommend good reads, as peer-group recommendation is the best way of encouraging others to read books.

This is an excellent opportunity to include stories written by people from all the cultures that may be represented by your class. www.literacytrust.org.uk/database/EALres.html provides a wide range of suggestions about books from other cultures. Paublo Books Limited specializes in multicultural fiction and non-fiction books from a wide range of publishers with a catalogue selected for Key Stage 3 and 4 and young adults (tel. 020 8422 7954, fax 020 8423 6713, email sales@paublo.demon.co.uk).

Insight into prejudice

Objectives targeted W7; TR6, 11, 18; SL**2**

Starter

Introduce the writer Alice Walker to the class. If they read 'The Flowers' in Year 7, remind them that this was also written by Alice Walker. Give every student a copy of the continuation of 'The Welcome Table' (**Worksheets 17a–b**). Again a quality reading of this story by the teacher will greatly increase the students' ability to tackle the related questions. Remind the students when they are listening to the story to focus on the structure of the story and the message the writer is trying to convey.

Introduction

For this final story, the students are not provided with a worksheet to help them with the analysis – this is in order to develop their ability to jot down appropriate notes independently. Encourage the students to use the Point, Evidence, Comment approach that they should by now be familiar with. They could draw up their own grid for this if it would help them. The paragraphs of the story have been numbered to facilitate feedback. An OHT of the second paragraph of the story would facilitate feedback on the final activity.

Differentiation

None of the five questions is easy but questions 1 and 2 are easier. You may wish to allocate these to groups who would find this activity difficult and then work with these groups. For the whole-class activity at the end of the introduction, reproduce the second paragraph of 'The Welcome Table' (top of **Worksheet 17a**) on an OHT to model for the class how to tackle the 'levels of meaning' activity – increasingly include the class in the activity. Encourage students to discuss their ideas in pairs before presenting them to the class. Able students could be stretched by being encouraged to lead some of the discussion on this paragraph.

Development

Model for the class how to sum up paragraph 1 as suggested in the Student's Book, and help the class jointly sum up paragraph 2. Write the finalized sentences on the board or OHT in flowchart form.

Teacher's notes

Divide the class into nine groups and allocate each group one paragraph.

Differentiation

The fact that the paragraphs have already been read to the class and that there has been considerable discussion of the story should help support this task. Paragraph 8 is the most difficult as well as the longest. The others are of roughly equal difficulty. Allocate the shortest paragraphs to groups that will find this task difficult.

Extended reading

It would be useful to have other stories, including short stories, by Alice Walker available for students who are interested in her writing.

Selecting your perspective

Objectives targeted W**3**; TW**5**

Starter

Encourage the students to use their whiteboards or a piece of paper to decide how they might group the spellings with appropriate advice to the Year 8 student on how to remember them.

Introduction

Outline the scenario from the Student's Book so that the students are clear about the sort of story they are going to plan.

Remind them of the stages they need to go through to plan their story and discuss a variety of the structural choices open to them, as well as a range of possible narrative perspectives as suggested in the Student's Book. Encourage them to use their whiteboards or spare paper to brainstorm ideas prior to sketching out the two most promising approaches, considering the advantages and disadvantages of each.

Development

When the students begin drafting their story using the perspective, structure and style that they think will work best, encourage them to give their story an appropriate title rather than just 'The Newcomer' which will suggest the story's purpose to the reader.

Plenary

At the end of the plenary session you may wish to read out the opening of one or two stories that are working well to help the students think about how they may redraft their stories for homework.

Extended writing

If these stories are developing well you may wish to extend the time being spent on this activity by changing the plenary to a pulling together of the problems confronted when planning such a story. The following lesson could then start with the plenary activity outlined above and the lesson could be used for redrafting the story effectively. This would allow more opportunity for guided writing. The homework could be replaced by the extended reading flagged on page 23.

Travellers' tales

Objectives targeted W5; TR11

Starter

Use the starter to introduce travel writing – the focus of the next five lessons. Give every student a copy of the continuation of 'Breaking into the Parthenon' (**Worksheets 18a–b**) and read the passage to the class. As with the short stories, a quality reading of this passage will greatly aid the students' ability to complete the following tasks.

Introduction

Divide the class into groups. Give every student a copy of the table about types of dictionary (**Worksheet 19**) so that they can sort out the highlighted vocabulary from **Worksheet 18a**. The students will need a range of specialist dictionaries to refer to. Make it clear to the class that these will have to be shared as it is only normal to have limited copies of such reference books. The fact that the passage has already been read to them should increase their ability to do this task.

Development

Divide the groups up into pairs. Give every pair a copy of the grid (**Worksheet 20**) to help them analyse the quality of the final paragraph (question 1). Inform the students to use their whiteboards or spare paper to jot down their points when they answer question 3. You may want to provide the pair whom you choose to lead the feedback on question 1 with an OHT of the final paragraph on which to present their points. Other groups could then add any additional points.

Similarly an OHT of **Worksheets 18a–b** would help the clarity of the feedback on question 2.

Extended reading

Liaise with the school library to supplement the

Teacher's notes

range of travel writing that is available for students to borrow to extend their reading in this area. A useful source of a range of travel writing is *Miles Ahead*, ed. Wendy Cooling, 2001 (HarperCollins).

Making an incident come alive pg 30–31

Objectives targeted W1; TR11

Starter [WS 21]

Present the opening paragraphs of the starter activity to the class. Allow students time to read the poem with a partner and select a volunteer to read the poem to the class. Explain about the homework and then give every student a copy of the irregular and regular verb grid (**Worksheet 21**). Model for the class how to complete this sheet and involve the class in this activity so that when they begin the work independently they are clear about what they are trying to do. This could be set as a paired activity.

Introduction [WS 22]

Give every student a copy of the extract 'Bicycle Buying in Hungary' from *Transylvania and Beyond* (**Worksheets 22a–b**) and introduce the story to the class as outlined in the introduction. Read it to the class. Again, a quality reading will greatly aid the students' ability to complete the tasks that follow. Remind the students to think about what they learn about Budapest from the story and what style the writer has chosen to use.

Development [WS 23]

Divide the class into pairs and give every student a copy of the question sheet on 'Bicycle Buying in Hungary' (**Worksheet 23**) to record their ideas. Tell each pair which question they should focus on so that they are prepared for the feedback session. Make an OHT of **Worksheet 23** so that students can refer to this when feeding back on the questions.

Differentiation

The easiest of the questions is number 4, possibly followed by numbers 3 and 6. These could be allocated to pairs who would have more difficulty with this work.

Homework

Remind the students of the homework that was set during the starter. They will need their filled in copy of **Worksheet 21** to provide them with some suggestions for verbs to use in their poem. Suggest that they use the opening two lines of the poem on page 30 to get them going. The purpose of this exercise is to encourage them to have fun with words while reflecting on regular verb patterns and the exceptions to the rule.

You may wish to set this as an optional homework. The whole point is to help students learn through playing with words. If the task is not enjoyable, it becomes self-defeating.

Perspectives on touring Britain pg 32–3

Objectives targeted TR9, 11

Starter [WS 24] [WS 25]

Use the information in the starter section to introduce the topic. Inform the students that they are about to compare Defoe's preface with Bryson's prologue so that they know what they are listening out for when they are read the passages. Then give every student a copy of the Defoe preface (**Worksheet 24**) and read it to the class, followed by Bryson's prologue (in the Student's Book, page 32). Divide the class up into groups and give every group a set of the cards from **Worksheet 25** so that they can sort them into statements that fit Defoe's preface and those that fit Bryson's prologue.

Introduction [WS 26]

Draw everyone's attention to the essay title on page 34 so that they know what they are listening out for when they are read the passages about Liverpool. Also tell them that they are going to be devising a comparison grid which will help them compare and contrast the passages. Give every student a copy of the Bryson extract about Liverpool (**Worksheet 26** – they already have the Defoe passage about Liverpool on **Worksheet 24**) and read both passages to the class.

The purpose of this activity is to build the students' confidence in devising their own comparison grids and thus their independence so that they do not become too reliant on the teacher to give them a way forward. The points that they sorted in the starter exercise give them significant help with this – so draw their attention to the 'Remember' box. If possible, turn **Worksheet 25** into an OHT and display it at this point. Advise them to use their whiteboards or spare paper to sketch out their ideas quickly.

In the feedback draw up a comparison grid on the board or OHP based on their suggestions so

Teacher's notes

that everyone has a coherent grid to be working on for their homework.

Development

The development activity focuses on the dominant feature of Bryson's travel writing – humour. It is preparatory work to help them sum up their points about Bryson's style when they write the essay in the following lesson.

Homework

The work students have done in this lesson should have provided the support to enable them to complete the analysis grid on their own for homework.

Differentiation

If it is felt that the homework is too difficult to do unaided, the spelling starter in the following lesson could be replaced with this activity.

Comparing Defoe's and Bryson's travel writing

Objectives targeted W**3**, 4; S4; TR9; TW17

Starter

Give every student a copy of the spelling strategies worksheet (**Worksheet 27**) and ask them to get out their spelling logs so they can decide which spelling strategies work best for them. You may want to get some students to feed back what words they have chosen, to help them devise strategies to secure their spelling.

Introduction

The main preparations have already been made for the students to write the comparison essay on Defoe and Bryson. Model for the class how to integrate evidence into effective sentences so that they feel more confident about making a point, supporting it with evidence and commenting further on the point. The more visual you can make this activity the more effective it will be. Blow up the phrases on **Worksheet 28** to a size that can be seen clearly from the back of the classroom and print out on card. If possible, present the sentence starters, linking phrases and supporting evidence on different coloured card – see grid on page 35 – as this will make the sentence structure visually clear. Manipulate your sentence strips so the class becomes confident in using a range of linking phrases. A pocket chart or fuzzy-felt board is ideal for this; alternatively use Blutack. The whole thing could be done on a board or OHT but using cards is more powerful because of their visual clarity.

Then ask the students to use the comment starters ('This is effective because …', etc.) to write sentences summing up the significance of the point being made. The purpose of this activity is to build up student confidence with using the formal language appropriate to comparison essays. In a later section of the book students will be required to complete such an essay in timed conditions (see pages 122–3). Use the example at the end of the introduction section to show students how integrate short quotations into sentences.

Development

Before the students start writing, make it clear how much time they have, what they should aim to complete in that time and at what time they will be told to read through their work. Remind the class they will need their completed comparison grids to help them with this essay. At the pre-stated time, ask the students to read through their work so far and annotate it with their suggested improvements.

Plenary

The students should swap their essays with a partner's and peer mark as suggested in the Student's Book.

Homework and differentiation

As suggested in the note on the previous lesson, the essay-writing task can be made easier if the spelling starter is replaced by filling in the comparison grid. The lesson time allocated to this spread could be doubled to allow more opportunity for teacher modelling and guided writing. If this choice is made, all the writing should be done in class time. The starter spelling activity could then become the homework for this lesson.

Writing your own traveller's tale

Objectives targeted TW6, 7, 11

Starter

Encourage each student to brainstorm a number of places that they have visited that have made a strong impression on them. Give every student a copy of the spider diagram (**Worksheet 29**) to help them work up the ideas that they associate with

Teacher's notes

this location. Use the example on page 36 to help them understand what they have to do.

Introduction

The introduction reinforces the routine that students should always go through when planning any writing – consider purpose, audience, form/structure. The activity helps them plan first the structure and then the style of their writing.

Development

Just before the students begin writing, remind them of the importance of beginning with an interesting paragraph that helps hook the reader.

Extended writing and differentiation

Again this activity could be extended over two lessons to give students longer preparation time and more opportunity for teacher modelling, guided writing and peer marking. If this choice is made, all the writing should be done in class time.

Plenary

The purpose of the plenary is to provide the students with good examples from their own work to reflect on so that they can consider ways in which their work could be improved. The plenary therefore has two parts and time should be provided to allow them to reflect on the quality of their work and annotate it so they know what to focus on when redrafting.

Reviewing what's been learnt

Apart from the suggestions in the Student's Book, you could also use the reviewing page to see if students have been encouraged to read travel writing as a result of this unit. If some students have found travel writing that they have enjoyed, allow time for them to explain why they liked it, as peer recommendations are the strongest way of encouraging reading.

Inform, explain, describe

Introduction

The lessons in the first part of this section introduce students to *Macbeth*, one of the set texts for Paper 2 of the Key Stage 3 NC Test. If your students will be studying this play for the test, then it would be useful to schedule the work in this section to fit in with your teaching.

The scenes chosen by QCA for particular study vary from year to year. In this section we have chosen Act 2 scenes 1 and 2, and Act 3 scene 4. If these are different from the ones being set currently, many of the activities will still be appropriate, as the tasks are to do with skills relating to writing about Shakespeare, as well as knowledge of the text as a whole. If you are studying a different Shakespeare text for the test, then you will need to adapt several of the activities to your chosen text.

The lessons and activities are intended to work alongside a reading/study of the text by the class. It will therefore be up to the teacher to judge when would be the most appropriate time for the individual lessons in the section. Further preparation for the Shakespeare paper can be found in a later section of Book 3 (pages 140–43).

The last five lessons of the section are devoted to an exploration and evaluation of the internet and the skills associated with finding, retrieving and using information using technology, leading to students creating their own website. If using the internet in your school is difficult due to a shortage of available resources, you may find it necessary to plan this section well in advance so that you can book your time when you need it.

The tragedy of Macbeth

Objectives targeted TR14

Plan ahead for this lesson by finding a suitable film or video production of *Macbeth*. Many schools find the BBC animated version is a good starting point as it gives a good outline of the story, themes and character development, and yet is only half an hour long. You may wish to show this to start with and then different, full-length versions later on. Depending on the version you show, the activities on these two pages could take longer than a single lesson.

Starter

This activity will help students to make the links between modern day attempts by producers to draw in the crowds to a production and what Shakespeare was doing in his time.

Teacher's notes

Introduction

The enduring popularity of Shakespeare's plays, and *Macbeth* in particular, should be emphasized and discussed. Active viewing of the video is encouraged: to enable students to respond to the questions on what they have seen, the teacher will need to stop the film at the end of every Act, apart from Act 4, which has been run together with Act 5.

Development

The sequencing activity is designed to reinforce the actions and events of the story. The cards on **Worksheet 30** will need to be prepared in advance. Having a secure knowledge of the narrative will help students to concentrate on the writer's purpose, character development, themes and language as they read the text.

Macbeth and history

Objectives targeted S11; TR15

Starter

Dividing the class into groups for these activities, with time for feedback, will enable some lively discussion about the nature of language change. The original meanings of the words in section C of **Worksheet 31** are as follows:

- batlet – the bat used to beat clothes in a wash tub
- gallow – to frighten
- pash – to smash
- mobled – muffled
- geck – a fool.

If you think the task is too difficult for your students as it stands, give them clues from the words above to help them. Credit should be given for the way in which they demonstrate their knowledge of how language develops, such as links with modern-day words/meanings, rather than simply 'getting it right'. You will find these, and other words, in *The Story of English* by Robert McCrum (Faber & Faber), p100. Another excellent source of information about language development, and Shakespeare's role in particular, is Bill Bryson's *Mother Tongue* (Penguin).

Differentiation

If you wish, students could be grouped by ability, as activities A to C become increasingly more difficult.

Introduction

This activity asks students to examine the nature of kingship. Understanding this concept will enable them to appreciate the downfall and evil of Macbeth and the nature of his tragedy. Students may find it helpful to look again at the sequencing of the story from the previous lesson to remind them of points they need to consider.

Development

It is easy to overlook the fact that there really was a king of Scotland called Macbeth. His rule in the eleventh century actually lasted for longer than Shakespeare gives him credit – 17 years. He was also not a bad king; in fact many positive points can be made in his favour.

Photocopy **Worksheet 32** and give a copy to each student. Comparing Shakespeare's version with a more accurate historical account, and thinking about why Shakespeare might have made the changes, will help students to appreciate the political nature of the play. Groups could be asked to examine different points, which will help to encourage a lively feedback session.

Shakespeare's imagery

Objectives targeted S7; TR14

Starter

Allow time for students to read some of their parodies of 'witches by e-mail' (**Worksheets 33a–b**). Updating Shakespeare in this way can be fun, but make sure they don't change the intended message of the original version or the point of the exercise will be lost.

Introduction

This lesson is concerned with the way in which Shakespeare creates an atmosphere of fear and the supernatural through the effect of his language and imagery. Read the speech on **Worksheet 34** to the class, bringing out its full impact. A video clip would also be useful.

Understanding the nature of a soliloquy as a dramatic device is important: students should consider the notion that the audience is seeing into the mind and soul of Macbeth, learning something about his private feelings rather than his public façade.

Development

In the second part of the speech, Shakespeare creates a vivid picture of horror through the strong imagery that he uses. Make sure that all students have a copy of **Worksheet 34**. The technique of highlighting and annotating key parts of the

Teacher's notes

speech is a useful practice which will help students to focus on the effect created through specific words and phrases. Encouraging the development of this skill will help them select points quickly in a test situation.

Differentiation

Some students might benefit from having some of the words already highlighted on their sheets as a guide. More able students could be asked to analyse and group the types of images that have been used, and consider why they have been chosen in particular, to bring out the connections with evil and the supernatural.

Interpreting a scene

Objectives targeted TR14; SL13

As this is a very active and vocal lesson, you may like to consider holding it in a drama studio or the school hall, where students have more room to move around.

Starter

Photocopy **Worksheet 35** onto cards and give one card to each pair. This activity gives students the opportunity to explore the different moods and characters that can be conveyed through the same words. If you have more than one version of *Macbeth* on video, you could demonstrate this point by showing contrasting representations of Macbeth and his wife (preferably not this particular scene).

Introduction

Give a copy of **Worksheet 36** to each student. If you have a mixed class, try to encourage mixed-gender pairs, with some girls examining Macbeth and some boys Lady Macbeth. It may produce some interesting results, particularly if in the development activity they join up with an opposite pair.

Differentiation

Assessing Lady Macbeth's mood is a more difficult task, particularly when considering the wider scope of her motives at this point in the play. Prompting some of your more able students in this direction should help to produce less predictable responses.

Development

Following the group discussion, students should be encouraged to move about, if they can, using the space and the physical distance between the characters to bring out the more dramatic moments

in this part of the scene. A good deal of meaning concerning the relationship between Macbeth and his wife can be conveyed through their body language as well as through the expression in their voices.

Shakespeare in performance

Objectives targeted S11; TR14, 15; TW11

Starter

Give each student a copy of **Worksheet 37** and get groups to discuss the questions in the Student's Book before feeding back to the class.

Introduction

Give each student a copy of **Worksheets 38a–b**. It would be useful to review Act 3 scene 4 before this activity, either by a close reading or watching the scene on video. Alternatively, members of the class could act out the scene to demonstrate what is happening visually.

Be prepared for the jigsawing activity here. Groups of four first need to be given one character to study; when their time is up they should re-form so that the new groups of four have one of each character, as far as possible. (Using the playing card method as described in Teacher's Resources Book 1, pages 143–4, may aid the organization.)

Differentiation

As Macbeth and Lady Macbeth have so much more to say, it might be better to give these characters to more able groups. Groups looking at the Lords and Banquo's ghost should be examining possible reactions and the significance behind their words and actions.

Development

Questions in the KS3 NC Test on Shakespeare in the past have asked students to step into the role of directors. This activity, apart from being interesting in its own right, also prepares students for such questions and helps them to think about other aspects of the play than the words alone.

Writing about Shakespeare

Objectives targeted TR14, 15; TW9, 10

Starter

Hot seating is a popular activity. It would help to give your chief characters time to consider their roles properly by warning them in advance.

Teacher's notes

Introduction [WS 39]

Examine the task set with the class by picking out the key words on the board, so that students do not lose sight of the focus. Gathering evidence from the text, using **Worksheet 39**, is a crucial part of the preparation. Point out to students the importance of direct quotation and close reference to the text.

The set time limit for the research activity is to help students to adjust to the idea of working to time, as they will need to do this in the test itself. Allow some time for feedback of the students' responses on **Worksheet 39** and the exchange of ideas.

Development [WS 40]

Planning is a necessary part of writing a good essay. Students must understand the need for effective planning and put this into practice. A planning frame has been provided here (**Worksheet 40**), but explain to students that there will not be one available in the test itself.

If you wish, the essay could be written not for homework, but in a follow up lesson, perhaps to time or under test conditions to help students prepare for the real thing.

At home on the web [pg 52–3]

Objectives targeted S8; TR4

The following five lessons are concerned with the nature of the internet as an information source. As the students will be asked to work in the same groups from now on to complete the final task – the creation of a website – it would be advantageous to plan the groups in advance. Ideally there should be five students in a group. They should, as far as possible, be equally mixed in terms of gender and ability. It would also be a good idea to ensure that there is at least one techno–wizard in each group, with a balance also of creative minds, organizers and speakers.

It would also be useful to have looked at the EPA site before this lesson.

Starter

Starting a collection of technological words for classroom display would be a valuable undertaking for some willing and helpful students. It is also interesting to examine the way in which these words have come into existence and their links with other words in our language. Never since Shakespeare's time, in fact, has there been such an explosion of new words.

Introduction [WS 41]

This activity asks students to explore and assess a website, focusing on its home page. The EPA site is well designed, clear and easy to use – though some may argue that there are far too many buttons and too much repetition. If possible students should investigate the site on screen. Check that they understand all the terms used, such as 'navigate' and 'hot link'. Give each student a copy of the evaluation sheet (**Worksheet 41**).

Development [WS 42]

The theme for the next series of lessons is the 'World at Risk', encompassing global warming, rainforests, whales and children's rights. The Student's Book will be using examples of websites concerned in particular with global warming as a demonstration model, while the groups will be developing their research skills using sites related to their chosen topic from the three others listed above.

Give each student a copy of **Worksheet 42**. Explain to students that they will be working together in these groups for the next few lessons. Decisions that they make now will affect what they do in the future; they won't have time to change their minds and do something different later on.

If the teacher does not feel comfortable with groups of students working on three separate topics then the choice could be limited.

Selecting and weighing up information [pg 54–5]

Objectives targeted S11; TR1, 4

Starter

The quantity and accessibility of information available on the internet is so overwhelming that it is important to help students develop some strategies that will enable them to select reliable sources. Anyone can put information on a website; there are few of the normal checks and verifications that are needed when something is printed in book form.

Introduction [WS 43]

Studying Paul Brown's article on global warming on **Worksheet 43** should help students with the process of selecting information. The specifically focused questions and the highlighting technique outlined in the flowchart should provide students with a 'way into' a text that involves scanning, skimming and accurate selection of necessary detail.

Teacher's notes

Differentiation

For students who would find this text too long and difficult, substitute one from the EPA 'Kids' site instead, and adjust the questions accordingly.

Development

Students should apply the same question and search method for their own website research material as they have practised in the introduction activity. Ensure that they have access to the internet when they undertake their research for homework.

How websites are structured pg 56–7

Objectives targeted S8; TR8; TW4

Starter

Ask the students if they can think of ways in which media texts are influenced by their readers as well as how they try to influence their readers. Have some daily newspapers, especially tabloid papers, available to illustrate how visual newspapers are becoming.

Refer the students to the picture of the EPA website on page 53 and divide the class into groups to discuss the questions. If possible, hold this lesson in a room with internet access so that every group can access the EPA site on line. This activity will be much more effective if they can interrogate the site and see how the different routes have been tailored to meet the needs of specific types of visitors to the site.

Introduction [WS 44]

As the students will soon be using the knowledge and information that they have found to create their own website, it is important that they learn how websites are constructed. (Try to use the terms 'construct' and 'structure' rather than 'design', as 'design' is better applied to the look of the page rather than the way it fits with other pages.) Give each student a copy of **Worksheet 44**, which demonstrates how the EPA website is constructed. If students have access to the internet during the lesson, they could explore the EPA site for themselves to help them understand the layers of pages and the connections and links between them. If this is not possible in the lesson, ask them to do this on their own later.

Development

Students should now be working in their groups to plan their own website on their chosen topic. It is important that they agree on the points listed in the Student's Book as the choices that they make now will affect their future work. Keeping things as simple as possible would be a good idea as time is short.

Plenary

Remind students that to be effective a website must be clear, well planned, easy to use and above all contain useful information. Students should complete their research for homework and bring their findings to the next lesson.

Creating your own web pages pg 58–9

Objectives targeted W**3**, 4; S8; TR**2**; TW4, 9, 12

Introduction [WS 45] [WS 46]

Read the panel and discuss the importance of the '4 As' as criteria for judging a website. Give copies of **Worksheets 45** and **46** to each student so that they can evaluate a particular web page using the criteria. Further information about evaluating websites can be found on the Yahooligans site, which has a good deal of other interesting and useful information and resources for teachers and students.

Development

Emphasis on the effectiveness of research techniques, as well as on content, is important when students create their own web pages. Asking them to submit their research printouts along with their web pages might help to deter the wholesale copiers of text. The group needs to work together closely if they are to avoid repeating information covered by someone else. Acting as proof readers, or critical friends, will also give them the experience of what it is like to produce material for a public audience.

Make sure that students focus on their individual web pages rather than the home page for their website as the latter will be done in the next lesson.

If the students are working on networked computers, and these computers are loaded with standard html software, each group can create their pages as they would appear on a website if they follow this procedure: (a) Save all the pages as html into the same folder; (b) Use the link and target facility to link the pages together.

Teacher's notes

The Website Challenge pg 60–61

Objectives targeted S8; TW4, **9**, 12

Starter WS 47 WS 48

Evaluating the examples of other home pages on page 61 and **Worksheets 47** and **48** is good preparation for creating and assessing the students' own work.

Introduction

Give students time to organize their contributions for presentation. They then need to work together to complete the final page of their site – the home page. Ask students why they think this page has been left until the end to be completed, rather than designed at the beginning. Groups should now put the pages of their website together. You may like to ask them to produce a site map to explain the links.

Development WS 49

Ask students to complete the evaluation of another group's work using **Worksheet 49**. It is better if group 1 does group 2, group 2 does group 3 and so on, rather than just swapping them over.

If students have been successful in completing this ICT project, it would be great to celebrate their success by asking a team of senior teachers to judge the completed work. Prizes could be awarded for the different aspects of the work such as team work, design, content etc.

Plenary

Draw together all the various skills that students have drawn on and developed in this section and celebrate the achievement.

Persuade, argue, advise

Introduction pg 63

A central purpose of the first unit of this section is to give students tasters of some great writers. The unit is also designed to build confidence in literary analysis. The second unit focuses on the rhetorical devices used by political parties to try to sell their politics.

John Donne, poet and preacher pg 64–5

Objectives targeted TR**12**, 15

Starter WS 50

Divide the class up into groups of no more than four. Give every group a set of the literary heritage cards (**Worksheet 50**) and explain the task as outlined in the Student's Book. Several of the writers focused on have already been included in Books 1 and 2 of *English Frameworking* to help build students' confidence. Most of the others have been selected because there is a strong chance that students would be familiar with them through films or musicals based on these texts. You may wish to use the feedback to establish the source of their knowledge.

Introduction

Introduce John Donne, relating him to his historical time as outlined in the Student's Book. Include any connections that can be made to work done in history since entering secondary school.

Go over the glossed words and phrases prior to reading 'The Sunne Rising' to help the students make sense of what they hear. Outline the three key questions that will be discussed as a class before the group work begins so they are clear what they are focusing on when they first hear the poem. A quality reading of the poem will help students complete the related tasks successfully. Discuss the first three questions as a class before allocating the different verses to different groups.

Differentiation

You may decide not to divide the class into groups but run the activity as a whole-class discussion to maximize the support that you can provide.

Development

Use the feedback from question 1 to illustrate the meaning of conceit.

Jane Austen, novelist pg 66–7

Objectives targeted TR15

Starter

You may wish to establish who is already familiar with Jane Austen through film or TV versions of her novels. If a significant number of students are,

Teacher's notes

you may wish to see if they can explain what Jane Austen may have meant by 'the little bit of ivory on which I work with so fine a brush'.

The purpose of the starter is to help the class understand the social context within which Jane Austen was writing so that the opening of *Pride and Prejudice* is meaningful. Use feedback to strengthen students' understanding of this context and also to build their confidence with applying word attack skills.

Introduction [ws 51] [ws 52]

This unit should help develop the students' literary analysis skills. Give every student a copy of the opening of *Pride and Prejudice* (**Worksheets 51a–b**) plus the related analysis sheet (**Worksheet 52**). Outline the questions the groups will be required to answer before reading the passage so that all are aware what they are focusing on.

Development

You may wish to ask students to briefly discuss each of the questions with a partner prior to the class discussion to maximize the range of contributors and help the less confident to contribute.

Charles Dickens, novelist pg 68–9

Objectives targeted TR15
Starter [ws 53]

Dickens is probably the best known of the writers focused on in this unit. Use the KWL grid to help establish what students already know about Dickens. Give every student a copy of the grid (**Worksheet 53**) and ask them to fill in the first column independently. Introduce the questions in the second column, which will be the focus of the development activity, so that each student is aware of the questions that the activities build up to.

Introduction [ws 54] [ws 55]

Get the students to feed back what they know about Dickens and integrate it into the introduction to Dickens outlined in the Student's Book. Bring out the contrast between Dickens' perspective and Jane Austen's.

Give every student a copy of the opening chapter of *Great Expectations* (**Worksheets 54a–c**). Set the scene of the novel's opening chapter, including the narrative perspective, before reading the extract. After reading the first chapter to the class, divide the class into groups, give each group a set of structure cards (**Worksheet 55**) and explain what they have to do as outlined in the Student's Book.

Development

Pull together the class's understanding of the passage through discussion of the questions listed in the Student's Book. All students fill in the final column of the KWL grid independently.

Advising film-makers

Objectives targeted TR10; TW15
Starter [ws 56]

You may wish to discuss the film version of *Harry Potter and the Philosopher's Stone* as a concrete example to illustrate the problems facing film-makers recreating popular novels. Divide the class into groups for the activity, give a copy of **Worksheet 56** to each student and ensure that whiteboards or spare paper is available.

Introduction

Show the class the opening section of at least one film or TV version of *Great Expectations*. All three film versions are easily obtainable. The Alec Guinness is arguably the best but its black-and-white old-fashioned appearance may undercut the exercise for some students. The Robert De Niro version is so far removed from the original as to perhaps cause confusion. The Michael York version or any of the more recent television versions may be the safest bet.

Tell the students to use the bottom half of **Worksheet 56** to note down their responses to the questions. Encourage them to do this in 'Point, Evidence, Comment' form. When the groups are feeding back, encourage the students to answer formally using the language of literary criticism. The more familiar they become with the patterns of such language the more easily they will be able to write them.

Development

Explain the task as outlined in the Student's Book, bringing their attention to the advice in the bullet points to help them set about the task. Use the bullet points as an example of the appropriate grammar and form of bullet points.

Plenary

Use the plenary to pull together the best of the

Teacher's notes

work from the development and to prepare for the homework.

Homework

Explain that work of a very high standard is expected for the homework since they have been given the opportunity to learn from others and redraft their work accordingly. It should be redrafted and proofread to a high standard so that there are no mistakes.

Coleridge, poet and essayist [pg 72-3]

Objectives targeted TR15

Starter [WS 57]

The purpose of the starter is to build students' confidence in using the terminology of literary criticism. Divide the class into pairs and give each pair a set of poetic terms to sort (**Worksheet 57**).

Introduction [WS 58]

Introduce Samuel Taylor Coleridge to the class along the lines suggested in the Student's Book. Give every student a copy of the extract from the poem (**Worksheet 58**). Outline the story of the 'Rime of the Ancient Mariner' so that the students understand the context of the poem since they will only be reading an extract from it. This is also a good opportunity to introduce symbolism, as suggested in the Student's Book.

Outline the task that the groups are going to be set before reading the poem. A quality reading of this passage will greatly assist the students' ability to analyse its literary ingredients. Stress that they don't have to limit their analysis to the terms from the starter activity – encourage them to use the blank cards to add to the points.

Development

Make an OHT of the extract from the 'Rime of the Ancient Mariner' to aid feedback from the groups who can add their points to the OHT.

Extended reading

The homework is a good opportunity to build on the reading targets set at the beginning of the year to expand the range of students' reading. Liaise with the school library or hold the lesson in the library to facilitate the recommending of books to students and to allow them to borrow them with ease. If possible, persuade your school library to get a copy of the 'Rime of the Ancient Mariner' as illustrated by Gustave Doré; this often fascinates students who are interested in art and is a good link with the art and poetry lesson that forms part of the 'Plan, draft, present' section later on (pages 116–17).

Politics as advertising [pg 74-5]

Objectives targeted W8; S6; TR7, 12; SL7, 9

Starter [WS 59]

Introduce Neil Postman's *Amusing Ourselves to Death* as outlined in the Student's Book. Divide the class into pairs and give each pair a copy of the text (**Worksheet 59**). Explain to the class before reading the passage what activity they will be doing so that they are ready to begin working as soon as you have finished reading and modelled how to annotate a paragraph.

Differentiation

This activity could be conducted as a whole-class activity with time for students to discuss issues in pairs to maximize confidence.

Introduction [WS 60] [WS 61]

Divide the class into groups of six and explain that these groups are to be subdivided into three pairs with each pair focusing on a different political party. Each group will need one copy of the opening of each party's manifesto (**Worksheets 60a–b**) and three copies of the analysis grid (**Worksheet 61**). Each pair should have a copy of the appropriate manifesto plus an analysis grid. Set a time limit for the pairs to complete their analysis.

Development

Each pair then feeds back their conclusions to the other pairs in their group and the group decides whether all three parties have used the same persuasive devices. Set a time limit on this activity so each group knows when the feedback to the whole class will begin.

When the time limit is up, select one group to present their conclusions to the class and see whether all the other groups agree. See if the class can come to an agreement about which parties used which techniques.

Plenary

See if the class has established sufficient evidence to support or refute Postman's contention that politics has become like advertising.

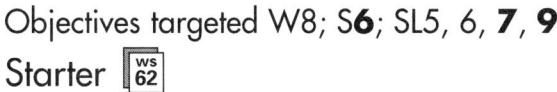

You may wish to extend these activities over two lessons to provide sufficient pair, group and class discussion time to enable the class to achieve a conclusion supported by evidence.

The politics of crime pg 76–7

Objectives targeted W8; S**6**; SL5, 6, **7**, **9**

Starter [ws 62]

Give every student a copy of the election briefing (**Worksheet 62**). Introduce the briefing and the related task as outlined in the Student's Book to help the students see the relevance of listening carefully. Read the briefing to the class, bringing out the way the article is structured. Allow time for the students to discuss each question briefly with a partner before feeding back. In the feedback on question 1, draw out the writer's use of a question as a heading for each paragraph which is directly answered by the opening sentence of each paragraph.

Make an OHT of paragraph 3 ('Have crime levels been rising…') so that feedback on the structure of the paragraph can be very focused. The structure of this paragraph provides a useful model for students to aspire to.

Introduction [ws 63] [ws 64]

Divide the class into three groups and explain that they will be working in pairs within these large groups. Give one group the Conservative Party's approach to crime, the second group the Labour Party's approach to crime and the final group the Liberal Democrat Party's approach to crime (**Worksheets 63a–c**). Give every pair a copy of the analysis grid (**Worksheet 64**). Tell them that each pair will rejoin their group after they have completed their analysis, just as in the previous lesson. Once the activity is under way, go round each group to help them select who is going to present their text to the class.

Development

Remind the class of the importance of being a good audience. Help the groups present their text as appropriate.

Letter to the editor pg 78–9

Objectives targeted S**3**, 4, 5, **9**; TR**12**; TW13, **14**

Starter [ws 65]

You may wish to present the main task of the lesson on an OHT. Divide the class into pairs and give every pair a copy of the newspaper letter (**Worksheet 65**). Draw the class's attention to the questions they will be answering on the letter before reading it to the class. Read the letter in the appropriate tone.

Introduction

Make sure every student still has their copy of the election briefing on crime (**Worksheet 62**) and whichever party statement on crime they have chosen to focus on. Remind the students of the purpose and audience of the letter they are to write and go over its content, structure and style as outlined in the Student's Book.

Development

Provide time here for the students to briefly rehearse their arguments with a partner – you may want to encourage them to get in role. The more they have thought through their arguments before they write, the easier it will be to write their arguments down.

Extended writing

You may wish to allow more time for the activity here. An additional lesson would provide more time for discussion and role play as well as time for guided writing and peer-group marking.

Interviewing techniques pg 80–81

Objectives targeted TW15; SL3

Starter

Introduce the task as outlined in the Student's Book. Read the Jeremy Paxman quotations in the appropriately belligerent tone of voice. Select a student to play Oprah Winfrey in the interview. You may wish to allow them some preparation time by giving them a photocopy of the interview in advance of the lesson so they can present the role effectively.

Before presenting the interview, explain to the class that they should focus on how the interviewer

Teacher's notes

has framed the questions and what effect this has on the answers given. Following the presentation of the interview, ask the class what type of questioning they find helpful or unhelpful. Draw out the 'dos and don'ts' of sympathetic interview technique.

Introduction

Divide the class into pairs and explain the task as outlined in the Student's Book. Each student will need their letter to the newspaper on crime to give to their partner.

Development

Get each pair to join up with a neighbouring pair. Each pair in turn then presents their interview to the other pair.

Plenary

Help the class refine the 'dos' of constructive interview technique.

Vote for me pg 82–3

Objectives targeted S**3**, **7**; TW4, 12, 13, 15

Starter

Divide the class into pairs and explain the task. You may wish to read the bullet point list to the class in the appropriate tone to speed up the activity, or to make it easier, or just to make it more entertaining.

Introduction

Present the task as outlined in the Student's Book. You may wish to get the class to brainstorm some ideas and put them up on the board to ferment ideas.

Development

Stress that this is a planning stage: only a rough draft of the leaflet is required. The final draft should be done for homework.

Analyse, review, comment

Introduction pg 85

This section consists of two units on two different genres – playscripts and journalism – but there are linking themes: the second unit begins with theatre reviews, which involves the students writing reviews of their own performances; and throughout the section there is an emphasis on attitudes to language, both spoken and written: this exploration of accent, dialect, Standard English and different formal registers culminates in a written analysis of slang in the final lesson of the section.

Attitudes to English in Pygmalion pg 86–7

Objectives targeted S10; TR14

Starter

The passage reproduced here is a combination of two extracts from Act 1 of *Pygmalion*. It provides the background to the main story and theme of the play as well as a peg upon which to hang a discussion on accent and dialect. It would help to point out that the play was written before the First World War when the gap between 'polite' and 'impolite' society (and accent) was much greater than it is today. You should take the part of Liza yourself – and practice in deciphering the phonetic pronunciation would pay dividends.

The use of the phonetic letter will provoke comment. Shaw was a tireless supporter of moves to reform the spelling of English to make it clearer and more logical. He left money in his will to fund the development of a new writing system on phonetic principles.

The questions on the passage are intended to lead students from the play itself to more general and topical issues around accent, dialect and Standard English. This is a highly complex area, which is revisited in later lessons in this section, so it is important not to get too bogged down in debate at this stage. Although both accent and dialect are referred to, they should not be used interchangeably: students should know that accent refers to pronunciation alone, whereas dialect describes a particular kind of English with its own pronunciation, vocabulary, grammar and idiom. Dialects are not only regional: as question 4 implies, any variety of English with distinctive vocabulary and grammar, whether based on region, class or profession etc, can be described a dialect. Question 5 may be answered in terms of 'appropriateness', but be prepared for more perceptive students to comment on wider issues of linguistic imperialism (it has been said that 'a standard language is a dialect with an army and a navy').

Teacher's notes

Introduction [WS 66]

Give every student a copy of **Worksheets 66a–b**. In the class reading of the scene you should take the part of Liza again, as the way in which she moves from over-polite salon English to Cockney dialect and back – but all packaged in exquisite enunciation – is critical for the meaning and impact of the scene. Make sure that you read the class the background information at the top of **Worksheet 66a**, and explain how such 'at homes' were highly rule-bound polite affairs in society at the time. There are nine parts altogether (plus one for the reader of the stage directions, who should be able to cope with several difficult words), so the reading alone should make for an entertaining class activity.

When students provide examples of very polite and formal Standard English (the second bullet point), you may like to ask them what makes each example polite or formal. This will require looking at the language more closely, as different examples have different characteristics, from inappropriately high register (Liza's weather report, lines 34–6), to the polite and formal use of such words as 'indeed' and the uncontracted forms 'is it not' (line 13) and 'I am going' (line 83).

Students may decide that Liza never reveals her Cockney accent (third bullet point), though they may also point to places where her guise slips for humorous effect, such as when she is taken by surprise (e.g. line 68). The important point, again, is to distinguish accent from dialect: Liza manages to conceal the former better than the latter, which provides much of the humour of the scene.

Development

Divide the class into five groups and allocate each group one of the questions to discuss. Give the easier questions 2 and 5 to groups that will struggle most with analysing a scene in this way. (If groups struggle with question 2, point them to the stage directions in lines 8–10.) Question 3 may elicit answers to do with slapstick humour, or with emphasizing how important it is for Higgins that Liza isn't exposed; these are certainly valid points, but Shaw is also making the more satirical and ironic observation that the well-to-do Higgins, obsessed with standards of English, is as clumsy and bad mannered as those he labels 'guttersnipes'. It may only be Liza who uses the expletive 'bloody' in this play (line 83), but Shaw has Higgins's housekeeper complain earlier in the play about his habitual bad language. Students may need to be helped towards appreciating how shocking this word would have been, not only in salon society but also on the early 20th-century stage.

Plenary

The plenary revisits the debate about Standard English highlighted in the starter. In fact Liza in the play complains that her new-found articulateness takes away her independence (she can no longer be a flower girl), but she does learn how to talk back to Higgins and not be treated like dirt by him, and eventually announces her intention of marrying Freddy.

Dramatic irony in The Rivals

Objectives targeted TR14; TW17; SL12, **13**

Starter [WS 67]

The analysis of *The Rivals* in this lesson focuses on dramatic irony; the starter activity is intended to get students thinking about how words can have layers of meaning, and specifically about how those layers can be revealed to an audience for dramatic effect. Copy and cut up the cards on **Worksheet 67** and give each pair a card. As the subtext relates only to the speaker of the opening line of dialogue, you could get each pair to swap round as they do their improvisations so that each student has a chance at hinting at the subtext. Draw attention to the bullet points in the Student's Book.

Choose pairs who have successfully revealed the subtext (without being explicit about it and 'giving the game away' to the other speaker) to perform their improvisation in front of the class, and ask the class if they can identify any of the ways in which the subtext is revealed. What effect (humorous or otherwise) is intended and achieved? In an alternative activity, you could ask the class to guess what the hidden thoughts of the speaker are – ensuring that other pairs who work from the same card keep quiet.

Introduction [WS 68]

There are some elements of continuity between Shaw's *Pygmalion* and Sheridan's *The Rivals* which you may like to point out: both are comic social satires, both make use of dramatic irony (in the scene analysed last lesson the audience and some of the characters knew who Liza really was, but the Eynsford Hills did not) and both have characters who struggle with language. Share some malapropisms with the class before reading the scene; just before Mrs Malaprop's opening line, for example, she praised Absolute as 'the very pineapple [pinnacle] of politeness'. You may like to take them through the misused grammatical terms in lines 10–13 and ask them what words they think she meant to use.

Teacher's notes

Photocopy **Worksheets 68a–b** and give each student a copy. Make sure that they understand the plot by reading and, if necessary, discussing the synopsis at the top of **Worksheet 68a** before you read the play as a class. Ensure that students know what dramatic irony is before you pair them for the activity. It may help to talk about it in this context as making the audience part of an in-joke against Mrs Malaprop. When the students have shared their examples of dramatic irony and discussed their effect you could ask them whether this technique could be used for non-comic effect. Reference to the Shakespeare play that they are studying may be helpful to draw out the tragic potential of dramatic irony; this will also be useful preparation for the improvisation and script-writing activities later in the section.

Development

Divide the students into groups of three: one is the director, one Mrs Malaprop and one Captain Absolute. The purpose of this activity is for the students to compare different interpretations of the scene by acting it out in two different ways, and to introduce students to working in a group with a director in preparation for the scripting and presentation activity at the end of the unit.

Comedies of manners are generally produced in the ostentatious manner described in the Student's Book; there is room, however, for alternative interpretations which have a different tone and bring out different aspects of the comedy. The better actors in the class should probably attempt the more naturalistic presentations; the director in these groups may need help in getting the actors to tone down their performance.

Homework

Ensure that students have a clear idea of the concept of dramatic irony before setting the homework. Remind them to 'flex their PECs' when citing evidence from the text, if necessary referring them to other places in the course where this is explained in more detail (e.g. page 34 in the Student's Book).

Directing a scene from Our Day Out

Objectives targeted S10; TR14; SL12

Starter

The second part of the starter (for which you need to photocopy the cards on **Worksheet 69** and give one set to each group) is a difficult activity as it entails discussing the characteristics of Standard English that make it the dominant mode of public communication. Remind students of the work they did on Standard English two lesson previously (page 87) and reinforce their understanding of what a dialect is. The term 'class' has deliberately not been used in the list of factors that contribute to different dialects, as we are all now apparently middle class, but you may like to use the term instead of 'social background' if it is appropriate.

The activity is not intended to present non-Standard English as 'worse' than Standard, but to reinforce students' understanding as to which contexts are more appropriate for non-Standard use, and to explore the reasons why one dialect has assumed such a powerful position. You may, however, like to plunge into more controversial waters by asking students if all the characteristics they identify make Standard English 'better' or just 'different'.

Differentiation

As this is a difficult activity you may wish to read through each of the cards in advance of the activity and make sure that students understand what they are describing. You could get more advanced students to give a short presentation explaining why Standard English is the dominant mode of public communication, using each pair of cards to give examples of what they mean (groups of six would allow one student to present each characteristic).

Introduction

Give each student a copy of **Worksheets 70a–b**. They should immediately relate to the language and theme of Willy Russell's play, and the discussion questions shouldn't present too much difficulty. Encourage students when they answer question 5 to think also beyond the practical point of Carol's decision not to jump, and to consider what is being said about human connection. It is Carol's 'reaching out' which allows Briggs to make a connection not only with her but with the more humane parts of himself: directors may choose to highlight this in different ways. (In the rest of the play he allows himself to enjoy the trip, and to be photographed enjoying himself with the children, though he reverts to type at the end when he deliberately exposes the film in his camera so that there is no record of his change of character.)

Teacher's notes

Development

Allocate a section of the playscript on the worksheets to each group (these would work: lines 1–12, 13–22, 23–34, 35–47, 48–60, 61–76); more than one group could work on each section, of course. Make sure that the groups read their section several times and discuss how to interpret it before annotating the script.

Plenary

If you have time you could get each group to present their lines in turn until the whole scene is covered. Are there any noticeable disruptions in continuity, where the interpretations are markedly different? Which are the most effective?

Writing a script pg 92–3

Objectives targeted SL12, 14

In this lesson groups improvise a scenario which acts as the basis for a script-writing activity; in the next lesson they will stay in their groups to rehearse and perform the scene, and evaluate the performances of other groups.

Starter

Divide the class into groups of five and outline the scenario to the class. If some groups have to be smaller than this you could dispense with the brother/sister. Make sure that students understand the terms 'crisis' and 'resolution' – refer them back to the scene from *Our Day Out* if necessary. The work of the director has already been touched on in this section, especially in the last lesson.

Introduction WS 71

Draw attention to the bullet points on page 93 to help the students focus their improvisations. You should be sensitive to the fact that the scenario may well reflect aspects of their own experience, present or past. Give every group a copy of the planning frame on **Worksheet 71** to help them record the details of the improvisation that works the best.

Development

Draw each group's attention to the steps outlined in the Student's Book in order to help them translate their improvisation into a script. Make sure that all students contribute and that all have a copy of the final script. An alternative approach to that outlined here is for the group to draft and redraft one copy collaboratively which is then photocopied once it has been finalized.

Additional time may need to be given to enable the groups to complete the scripts to their satisfaction.

Plenary and homework

The plenary discussion is one means of ensuring that groups are on the right track as far as the central purpose of the scenario is concerned. Tell students that they will be rehearsing and performing their script next lesson, so the more they can familiarize themselves with their part for homework the better.

Evaluating the performances pg 94–5

Objectives targeted SL11, 14, 15

Starter

The purpose of the starter is to free students up for the acting that is the main focus of the lesson. It's also great fun. Follow the instructions as outlined in the Student's Book. Encourage students to get into their performance as wholeheartedly as possible: it is more important that they do this than that the volunteer guesses the adverb.

Introduction

The introduction allows the students time to rehearse their scene. Draw the groups' attention to the bullet points in this section to help them focus on making their presentation effective.

Development WS 72

Give every student a copy of the self-evaluation grid on **Worksheet 72** to help them reflect on the quality of the performances. Remind them to keep their worksheet, as they will need to refer to it in the next two lessons of the section.

Plenary WS 73

Give every student a copy of the self-evaluation grid on **Worksheet 73**. Allow more time than usual for the plenary, as this is an opportunity for students to evaluate their involvement in drama activities throughout the year, and to set targets for improvement.

Teacher's notes

Looking at listings pg 96–7

Objectives targeted W6; S3; SL15

Starter ws 74

Copy **Worksheet 74** and give a set of cards to each group. As the categories of formality are not completely distinct, but often overlap one another, students may struggle to distinguish one type of informal language from another. Encourage them to use the diagram in the Student's Book, to arrange the non-formal words in order of formality: the most informal phrases will tend to be the slang examples. Tell them that 'colloquial' relates to conversations, that is, spoken rather than written language; this will help students distinguish colloquial from informal words. You should not be too prescriptive, however: there is room for argument, and much depends on the context.

The final part of the activity is intended to get students to think about context and appropriateness. If they find it difficult to think of situations in the abstract, get students to look at the words they have categorized and ask them in what situations they would use them.

Introduction ws 75

Get students to see that some listings are mini-reviews, and to look closely at the text to analyse what it is that might persuade readers to go to the performances. As so often, these texts combine a number of purposes: to persuade (the review element), to inform (the listings element) and to entertain (they are little art forms in their own right).

Display the first listings entry on **Worksheet 75** as an OHT and show the class how to analyse the vocabulary, grammar, structure and style. Emphasize the purpose of each of the features: the condensed, abbreviated style of the noun phrases, for example, not only allows the entry to take up less space; it also gives the entry a unified slick and snappy feel. Then get students to annotate the second entry in a similar way; ask those who need help to consider the use of brackets, the purpose of all the references to TV, the emphasis on personalities, and the grammatical type of the first sentence (compound, which allows you to add further details easily by tagging on phrases and clauses with conjunctions and prepositions). Choose some pairs to present their analysis by displaying it on an OHT and talking through the points they have made.

Development ws 76

Copy **Worksheet 76** for each student, and make sure they have their completed copy of **Worksheet 72** to refer to. Encourage students to be positive about the performance that they are writing about in case the exercise is used as a way of attacking other students. If you are worried about this you could ask them to do an entry for the group that they awarded the highest mark.

Plenary

This is an opportunity not only to hear some of the best writing but also to revisit the issues of context and appropriateness of language that were floated in the starter activity.

Reviewing a review

Objectives targeted S2, **3**, **9**; TR**7**; SL15

Starter

There are at least four important functions of punctuation: to show the grammatical structure of text so that it can be read coherently, for example by using full stops and commas; to represent the intonation and emphasis of spoken language, for example through the use of question marks and parentheses; to highlight the structure of complex sentences (use of semi-colons and colons); and to add a nuance to the meaning, for example through the use of 'scare quotes' to show that a word has a special sense. All of these functions are represented in the passage that the students are asked to analyse, although at this level you may wish to look no further than the single portmanteau answer 'to clarify meaning'.

The semi-colons in the extract are used to separate complex points in a list and thereby give a manageable structure to the sentence. If students are unsure about this, ask them how clear the sentence would be if commas alone were used.

Introduction ws 77

Give each student a copy of **Worksheet 77**. Read the review to the class before dividing the students into groups to analyse it. Question 6: the final sentence ('Fairly magical, indeed') refers back to the opening sentence and combines this ring composition with a feeble pun on the title of the musical; whether these devices make it an effective ending to the review is a matter for debate, but you could make the point that they are devices commonly used in all sorts of journalism.

Teacher's notes

Development

An alternative activity, if you feel that the student performances have already been reviewed to death, would be to write a review of the school play, or of a play that the whole class has seen recently as part of a class trip. If they do review the student performances, make sure they have their copy of **Worksheet 72** to refer to. The bullet points remind students to cover all three aspects of script, direction and acting. You should encourage the less able to devote one paragraph to each of these aspects in their review, and the more able to give their review a more interesting structure. Ask students how formal their writing should be, given that the audience will be readers of an upmarket local paper, and contrast this with the relative informality of the listings entry they composed last lesson.

The celebrity interview

Objectives targeted S**3**, 4; TR3; SL3

Starter

The aim of this teacher-led activity is to get students thinking about the different ways in which they could speed up their note-taking. As well as the symbols on the notice board, you could ask students what ordinary abbreviations they use, or could use, such as 'Weds' for Wednesday. Making up an abbreviation for a word that is constantly used can also save a lot of time, e.g. 'Sh' for Shakespeare.

The text message on the mobile phone reads 'Be seeing you tonight'. Other potentially useful abbreviations that are commonly used in text messaging are: C (see), COZ (because), NE1 (anyone), PLS (please), R (are), U (you). Even if many of these (and others that students will inevitably come up with) may not be useful for the kind of note-taking they have to do at school, it makes the point that a vast number of words can be abbreviated; also, as students are the only ones reading the notes, it doesn't matter if a private language is used.

Introduction

Give each student a copy of Tony Parsons' interview with Victoria Beckham (**Worksheet 78**). Question 2: the topical context/reason for the interview is given in paragraphs 5 and 6.

Development

Give each student a copy of **Worksheet 79**, to help them consider important issues of structure and style before they draft their article.

Analysing an analysis

Objectives targeted S5; TW10

Starter

Give each student a copy of **Worksheet 80**. This activity is intended to get students thinking in detail about how they would create sentences and link them together to create a cohesive paragraph which follows one idea through logically. This is, in part, preparation for when they write their own analysis article next lesson. Encourage students not merely to rewrite the bullet points as grammatical sentences, but also to link them together in an elegant and effective way through connectives.

You may like to get the students to construct their paragraphs on screen; this variation would be facilitated if the bulleted information is already keyed in for them.

This was the original paragraph (from *The Week* magazine):

Have sharks always inspired terror?

In the fifth century BC the Greek historian Herodotus noted that they were man-eaters, and they have terrified seamen ever since. But strangely enough, at the turn of the last century, there was a conviction that sharks were harmless. In 1891, a US millionaire called Hermann Oelrichs offered $500 to anyone who could prove that a shark had ever attacked a human being; and in 1915, a New York Times editorial, entitled 'Let Us Do Justice to Sharks', argued that sharks were timid creatures with feeble bites that could never sever a human leg. Such perceptions changed dramatically the very next year when a Great White shark went on the rampage off the coast of New Jersey, killing four and tearing both legs off one victim. This sparked the first recorded outbreak of shark hysteria and was the inspiration for Peter Benchley's bestselling novel *Jaws*.

Introduction

Having practised shaping sentences into a single cohesive paragraph, students are now required to analyse how several paragraphs may be combined in an effective way in a whole article. Copy **Worksheet 81** and give one to each student. Read the instructions at the top of the worksheet before dividing the class into pairs. The first two paragraphs of the article combine purposes 1 and 2; paragraphs 3 and 4 focus on news/explanation; paragraphs 5–8 analyse the underlying issues;

English Frameworking 3: Teacher's Resources   © HarperCollins*Publishers* 2002

Teacher's notes

paragraph 9 is something of a lighthearted sign-off, but is arguably purpose 1; the quotes in the display box provide further evidence for purpose 2.

Development

Students now discuss aspects of the language and style of the article. They will revisit these issues when they come to compose their own analysis article next lesson.

Analysis: Is slang cool?

Objectives targeted S4, 5, **9**, 10; TW**9**, 10, **16**

Starter

The starter activity gets students thinking about the term slang, a definition of which is provided at the top of **Worksheet 83**. The 'special vocabulary' meaning of slang (meaning 3 in the dictionary entry), which stems from its prime function as a tool to define an in-group, has been flagged in the description of slang already given on page 96, and it is referred to later in Tony Thorne's statement on the worksheet. At this stage, however, you may be satisfied with a definition that focuses on 'highly colloquial language'.

Students may point out that the government report was controversial not only because it made informal language as acceptable as formal language in exams (a formal context), but also because the report itself crossed this boundary by using an inappropriate register in places.

Introduction

As preparation for writing their own analysis article on slang, students are asked to recall everything that they have already learnt in the last few lessons about slang, discuss this and jot down their thoughts on **Worksheet 82**, a copy of which should be given to each student. Then give each student a copy of **Worksheet 83** and ask groups to read and discuss the views expressed. Make sure that the factor of appropriateness is understood in the feedback.

Development

Before students begin to draft their article, read the advice in the display panel to the class, and point out both the title and the word length that the article should have. You could encourage students to highlight those opinions on **Worksheet 83** that they want to quote as evidence in their article. Get students to peer assess each other's drafts before the end of the lesson.

Differentiation

You may wish to give less able students only the last three statements on the worksheet, if you feel that they may be overwhelmed by too much material; however, if you exclude **Worksheet 83** altogether students are not provided with any viewpoints to represent or quote in their article.

Plenary

Use the plenary session to ensure that students are on the right track before asking them to redraft their articles for homework.

Plan, draft, present

Introduction

The writing objectives for Year 9 lack any objectives that focus on the enjoyment that expressing yourself creatively can bring. A central purpose of this section is to meet all the required 'Plan, draft, present' writing objectives as well as adding in this creative writing element. Poetry has been selected as the medium for this since it is the perfect form for creative writing as well as suiting formal essay writing and presentation. The poems have been selected for the quality of their expression and ideas, and for the range of their form and style. There is no attempt to cover the full range of poetic form but rather the emphasis is on covering a range of ways of expressing human hopes and fears and the experiences that inspired them.

Quality of discussion is vital to the success of this section, thus the students are encouraged to value speaking and listening through a formal process of evaluation which runs throughout the section. The section also ends with an oral presentation of poetry to help students build confidence in talking about poetry, since the formulation of coherent ideas underpins successful writing. To support systematic thinking about how to analyse poetry, an analysis template is introduced in the first lesson and then repeatedly used in subsequent lessons so that students become familiar with the type of points to bear in mind when analysing poetry and preparing for formal writing about poetry.

Teacher's notes

Throughout the section it is suggested that the teacher reads the poems to the class initially, since it is impossible to read these poems well on sight, and the quality of the reading will greatly help the students hear the quality of the poetry. The presentation lessons give the students the opportunity to read these poems out loud once they have got their heads round their meaning.

Wishing your life away

Objectives targeted TR17; TW8

Starter

This activity can lead to fascinating discussion about the human condition. If you do not want the students to write their chosen age on whiteboards, an alternative method is to get everyone to close their eyes and then give instructions like 'Put up your hand if your selected age was between 16 and 20' and so on. You can then sum up the outcome for the class. The whiteboards have the advantage of providing an instant visual picture on which to base the forthcoming discussion. Trying to get each student to think privately about this question helps the quality of the ensuing discussion. Most students will probably select to be a few years older than they are now. Whatever their choice is, ask them to justify this choice.

Then ask them if, when they reach their chosen age, they will be happy to be that age. You will probably find that they instantly respond no, they will want to be a different age. Allow the discussion to develop to tease out whether human beings have a tendency to be dissatisfied with what they have now and always want for something different. Tease out at what age they will start wanting to be younger and why.

If some students have selected a younger age than themselves, draw out the reasons why.

Introduction

'Rising Five' has been selected because of the quality of the poem's diction, imagery and sound effects as well as its theme of life turning into death as part of the natural cycle. The notice board of possible ingredients is there to help students think about the range of aspects they should be looking for when analysing poetry formally. This notice board has been reproduced on **Worksheet 84** for use as an OHT or for being blown up into a poster to support work throughout this section. Selecting evidence to support these ingredients provides informal practice in flexing their PECs – selecting the point, supporting evidence and related comment.

Differentiation

Ensure students have a chance to discuss the questions informally with the person sitting next to them before the whole-class discussion, to maximize participation and allow unthreatening thinking time. All students can join in the discussion on the quality of the imagery in this poem if it has been well read to them.

Development

The opening discussion followed by the quality of 'Rising Five' should help students to have ideas about what they want to express about their feelings about age. The form of the poem has been left open; there are no restrictions on the students' creative expression on this issue.

Plenary

The plenary questions are there to help the students recognize how the nature of poetry makes it the perfect medium for expressing the central concerns of human beings.

Extended writing

No formal homework has been set but this is an excellent opportunity to encourage those who felt inspired by this topic to develop their thoughts.

Sonnet form

Objectives targeted S3; TW8

Starter

The purpose of this starter is to strengthen the students' understanding of sonnet form rather than to do a close analysis of this particular poem. A Shakespearean sonnet has been selected as a classic example of the genre. Sonnet 138 has been chosen rather than sonnet 55 (which Wendy Cope parodies in her poem, and which is presented on page 32 below for those who wish to make a direct comparison), since it is more accessible and is particularly good as an example of Elizabethan wit. The technical information in the information box can be referred to if appropriate to help students understand the formality of the sonnet form. The rhythm of sonnet form may need drawing out.

Teacher's notes

> **Sonnet 55**
>
> Not marble, nor the gilded monuments
> Of princes, shall outlive this pow'rful rhyme,
> But you shall shine more bright in these contents
> Than unswept stone besmeared with sluttish time.
> When wasteful war shall statue overturn,
> And broils root out the work of masonry,
> Nor Mars his sword nor war's quick fire shall burn
> The living record of your memory.
> 'Gainst death and all oblivious enmity
> Shall you pace forth; your praise shall still find room
> Even in the eyes of all posterity
> That wear this world out to the ending doom.
>   So, till the judgment that yourself arise,
>   You live in this, and dwell in lovers' eyes.

Introduction

Each group will need a set of the lines from Wendy Cope's sonnet cut into prose strips (**Worksheet 85**) plus a pair of scissors so they can cut the strips appropriately. Blow up the correctly laid out poem from the bottom of the worksheet so that it can be used as an OHT to support feedback from the exercise. Alternatively use the strips as an OHT so that a group can demonstrate how they arranged the lines. They could also read the poem in the appropriate tone. The purpose of this sorting activity is to help the students grasp the nature of sonnet form before attempting to write their own. Point out the diction of the poem so that the students can see how the sense of one line flows over into the next rather than ending with the rhyme. Awareness of this may help them with the problems of getting their sonnet to rhyme.

Differentiation

This task is easier if you read the sonnet to the class before they attempt to establish the line form.

Development

The Wendy Cope sonnet was selected to provide an unthreatening template to help scaffold students' attempts at writing within sonnet form. The suggestion that students use the opening words and closing rhyme to help them write their sonnet may help some to get going.

Differentiation

The whole purpose of this is that the students should enjoy trying to write within sonnet form rather than feel oppressed by it. Students who have difficulty with this may want to rely heavily on Wendy Cope's pattern of language.

Poems don't have to rhyme

Objectives targeted TW2, 8; SL1, 4, 8

Starter

The starter establishes the centrality of discussion to this section and gives it the formal status of reading or writing, since there is a tendency for students to think that talking can't be working. Give every student a copy of the evaluation sheet (**Worksheet 86**) on which to write the targets for the coming section, as well as their speaking and listening record (**Worksheets 87a–b**, printed back to back on one sheet). Stress that you expect every student to contribute to whole-class discussion by the end of this section. Throughout the section, attempt to spread contributions out so that by the end of the section everyone has contributed more than once to whole-class discussion. Keeping a simple record of who has contributed to whole-class discussion in the register can be useful as a way of preventing class discussion from being dominated by a few students.

Introduction

The focus of this lesson is to enthuse children with the appeal of William Carlos Williams' poems so that they are inspired to write their own poems about everyday topics using a similar opening. Read 'This Is Just To Say' to the class and encourage the students to discuss in pairs what makes it effective. Use the class discussion as a springboard to help them write their own short poems about apologizing for something that they are secretly pleased that they did. Read some of the resulting poems to the class.

Development

Then read 'The Red Wheelbarrow' and get the class to discuss what difference the way the poem is broken into lines makes to its meaning. Ask the class to discuss what makes this poem effective. Using the opening line 'So much depends', get the class to write their own simple short poems using a similar line pattern to Williams'. Then get the students in groups to choose the most effective of the poems to present to the class.

Teacher's notes

Plenary

Each group presents their chosen poem to the class. Ask the students to fill in the first section of their speaking and listening record (**Worksheet 87a**). Remind the students to keep this speaking and listening record, as well as the evaluation sheet (**Worksheet 86**), in a safe place since both will be needed in subsequent lessons.

Make a display of the best of the poems produced and add to it throughout the section.

Playing with syntax pg 114–15

Objectives targeted W6; TW4, 8

Starter

Read 'According to My Mood' by Benjamin Zephaniah to the class. You may wish to reproduce this on an OHT to help focus the discussion feedback and to draw attention to the presentational devices used.

Introduction ws 88

Read 'anyone lived in a little how town' (**Worksheet 88**) and ask the class for their first impressions. The development session allows time for a more in-depth discussion following analysis of each verse so the emphasis here should be on class's first impressions.

Development ws 89

Divide the class into eight groups and give each group one verse of the poem to focus on (**Worksheet 89**) plus an OHT of the same verse to annotate and present once the group has finalized its ideas.

Model for the class how to annotate their verse along the lines suggested in the Student's Book. Encourage the groups to hazard a guess as to why Cummings has selected the words that he has in the lines that break the rules of grammar.

The discussion following the verse by verse analysis could possibly be achieved without reference to the poetry analysis notice board (**Worksheet 84**) since the key points should already have been established.

Differentiation

This activity can be made easier by being conducted as a class activity with the teacher doing the annotating to suggestions from groups. The teacher can also work with those groups that would find this activity most difficult. However, the repetitive nature of the poem means that many of the points that are relevant to verse 1 also appear in a slightly different form in subsequent verses, so much depends on the modelling at the beginning of the activity.

Inspired by art pg 116–17

Objectives targeted TR7, 17

Starter

You may wish to liaise with the art department prior to this lesson to see what artists the students would be familiar with in order to maximize the effectiveness of this activity.

Introduction ws 90

Give each student a copy of the poem on **Worksheet 90**. Before beginning the poem you may like to show the class some additional Brueghel paintings which will help the students comprehend the images in the opening verse.

Allow the students time to discuss the questions following the poem to help build up confidence and extend the range of people willing to contribute. Display the poetry analysis notice board (**Worksheet 84**) to help the students answer question 2 on the ingredients Auden has employed.

Development ws 91 ws 92

Give every student a copy of **Worksheets 91** and **92**. When the students are feeding back their ideas ensure that the multiple narration of 'Not My Best Side' is brought out, including the different language patterns used by each narrator.

Differentiation

This lesson can be made easier if only one poem is covered in the development activity. If 'Not My Best Side' were selected, different groups could be asked to feed back on different verses to bring out the range of narration in this poem.

Expressing grief pg 118–19

Objectives targeted TR7, 17; TW4

Starter

Divide the class into groups of no more than four students. Given the sensitive nature of the theme of these poems, consideration may need to be given to the composition of these groups.

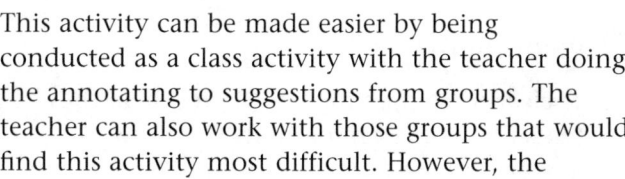

Teacher's notes

Introduction

Display the poetry analysis notice board (**Worksheet 84**) to help students analyse the ingredients of both poems. In the discussion bring out the significance of diction in the poems. Both poems work well with students of all abilities and can be appreciated at a range of levels.

Development

The theme for the students' own poems has been deliberately widened to include any strong feeling so that no student is pressurized into focusing on personal grief. Students who wish to avoid expressing their own feelings directly are also given the autobiographical style route. The students have now experienced a wide range of forms and styles and are free to choose those best suited to their aims and inclinations.

Homework

The homework fulfils a range of purposes; this includes allowing students to celebrate and present the best of their work which can then be displayed in the classroom. This work can be drawn on by groups for their presentations at the end of the section.

Preparing to write an essay

Objectives targeted TR7, 17; TW2, 3

Starter

Give every group the list of preparations on cards (**Worksheet 93**). A logical order is presented on the worksheet before it is cut up. 'Re-read the question carefully' would be appropriate in a range of places. The important thing is that the students know that they should always check that they are interpreting the question correctly before finalizing their plan for answering it. It is easy to misinterpret a question and go off in the wrong direction.

Introduction

Read 'Death of a Naturalist' to the class. Give every student a copy of the analysis grid (**Worksheet 94**) which should be familiar to the students since it is the same framework as they have been using throughout the section when analysing the ingredients that poets have used. Model for the class how to begin filling this in, then scribe for the class as they suggest how it could be filled in. Students should fill in their grid at the same time. You may wish to fill in 'author's purpose' last as this is often the most difficult aspect and is easier once you have analysed the rest of the poem.

Development

Give each student a copy of 'In Mrs Tilscher's Class' (**Worksheet 95**) and read it to the class. Give every student a copy of the analysis grid (**Worksheet 96**) – which, except for the poem's name, is exactly the same grid as they filled in earlier – to help them compare the poems.

Differentiation

Additional help can be given to the students by increasing the extent of the modelling in the introduction activity. In the development the student feedback could be pulled together by the teacher who leads the filling in of the analysis grid.

Comparing two poems

Objectives targeted S4, 5, **9**; TR**7**, 17; TW1, **3**

Starter

Give every group a set of sentence openers to sort (**Worksheet 97**). This exercise serves the double purpose of reinforcing the appropriate level of formality for this essay while providing potential sentence starters to help students set off in the right direction.

Introduction

Talk the students through the advantages and disadvantages of the two possible structures for this essay. Approach 2 is often seen as being better but it is harder to control. It is important to ensure that the reader has a strong sense of what both poems are about and their style – this can be lost when switching from poem to poem to bring out points of comparison or contrast. On the other hand, approach 1 can sometimes lead to a boring repetition of what the poet said and lack sufficient analysis and comparison. The most important thing is that the students know that they must plan what they are going to write before they start writing and that it is necessary to decide on the overall structure that the essay will take. Excellent essays can be written using both approaches.

Development

Make clear what the time limit is and help the students follow the timing hints from the display panel.

Teacher's notes

Homework

Provide every student with a copy of **Worksheet 98** to help them analyse their writing skills and set targets for future development.

Organizing group presentations

Objectives targeted TW4; SL10

Starter

Give every student a copy of **Worksheet 99** to establish which poems they each preferred. The opening lines, title and author of each of the poems are in the Student's Book to remind them of the poems they have studied. The extract from the 'Rime of the Ancient Mariner', which they studied on pages 72–3, could be added to the list. Ensure that each student puts their name on their sheet.

Introduction

Divide the class up into groups of no more than four. Make certain all the groups understand the problem that they are trying to solve – see the bullet points in the Student's Book. A possible solution to the problem is as follows:

- Give each student three strips of paper which they use as follows:
  1. Write your name and poem of 1st choice on strip one
  2. Write your name and poem of 2nd choice on strip two
  3. Write your name and poem of 3rd choice on strip three

- Sort all the strips of paper by title of poem.

- Sort the names for each poem into 1st, 2nd and 3rd choice.

- Look at all the first choices and create up to two groups of 3/4 people for each poem selected. Separate people who normally work together if there is more than one group.

- Remove the 2nd and 3rd choice slips of the people who have been allocated their first choice.

- Go through a similar process with the 2nd choices.

- Top up or establish new groups with 3rd choices.

If the groups do not come up with a feasible solution, see if they can put the above into practice.

Development

Divide the class into the groups established in the introduction activity. Explain to the groups what their task is and go over the rules of the exercise.

Plenary

Draw up the class's 'dos and don'ts' so they can be displayed to help support the next lesson.

Presenting a favourite poem

Objectives targeted TW2; SL1, 4, 8, 10

Starter

Reassemble the groups that were working on the presentations at the end of the last lesson. Remind the groups of the guidelines for successful presentation and establish how much preparation and rehearsal time the groups have.

Introduction

Set up the classroom so that it is suitable for the groups to present their chosen poems. Give each student a copy of the evaluation grid (**Worksheet 100**) and ensure they are clear about how to fill it in. Remind the class about the importance of being good listeners. If more than one group is presenting the same poem, separate out their presentations.

Development

The students will need their speaking and listening record sheets (**Worksheets 87a–b**) and their initial evaluation grid (**Worksheet 86**), as well as **Worksheet 101**, to complete their evaluation of their speaking and listening. You may prefer not to use **Worksheet 101** but rather get the class to amend **Worksheet 86** to see if they would change anything given their performance in this section.

Teacher's notes

Preparing for NCTs and looking ahead to GCSEs

Introduction [pg 129]

Although this section comes at the end of the Student's Book, the NCT lessons would obviously need to be taught in March, April or May in order to prepare students for their tests. The first part of the section covers exam preparation as well as practice for Papers 1 and 2. It is designed to help students to understand both the nature and the purpose of the tests. The last three lessons of the section aim to introduce students to the requirements of GCSE and to help them prepare for what is to come by setting further targets as well as independent reading challenges to be undertaken during the summer holidays. It is probably best to do this work towards the end of the summer term.

The section as a whole encourages a positive attitude towards formal testing as a way of emphasizing the success and achievement of students at this stage of their education, providing them with encouragement and helping them to feel proud of their accomplishments.

Getting into training [pg 130-31]

Starter

Begin by asking students what they feel about taking tests before reading the text. Try to maintain an 'upbeat' approach to dispel nerves and tensions at this stage. Tests are simply a fact of life and it is better to face them head on and prepare for them properly than to pretend that they won't happen. Allow time for feedback, particularly responses to the second question, which could be written up and displayed in the classroom.

Introduction [ws 102]

It is helpful to establish the nature and content of the tests, so that students fully understand what is expected of them. Give each student a copy of **Worksheet 102** and talk through the detail. Emphasize in particular how many questions they will need to answer and the time to be spent on each. (It will be useful to reiterate this throughout the section and again just before each paper.) In the feedback session ask students what they can do to overcome their main concerns.

It is worth pointing out that there are several differences between this end of Key Stage 3 test and the optional tests students may have taken in Years 7 and 8, particularly with regard to the number of questions they need to answer and the organization of the two papers. Discuss these differences now to avoid misunderstandings later.

Development [ws 103]

Give a copy of **Worksheet 103** to each student. Begin by asking students how much they already know about NC levels. The word box on page 131 provides a definition, as well as target expectations, for students at the end of Key Stage 3. It is important to stress that these are average targets and that each student should have a personal goal that is appropriate to their ability.

Most teachers find that it is helpful to give students as much information as possible about assessment criteria as it helps to guide students towards the right type of responses. However, ensure that the difficult words and phrases, such as 'identify', 'convey', 'inference' and 'deduction', in the criteria are explained clearly in terms that students understand. Talking about what these terms mean will help to establish the skills that students need to acquire in order to progress through the levels described.

The order of the statements and levels is as follows:

Response to non-fiction and media texts
G   level 6
H   level 4
I   level 8
J   level 5
K   level 7

Response to literature
L   level 7
M   level 8
N   level 6
O   level 5
P   level 4

Differentiation

The statements themselves have been drawn from the level descriptors at the back of the English National Curriculum document. If you think it would be helpful, this could be copied for students to use during or after the task.

Plenary

If you wish, ask students to write what they need to do in their work planners or homework diaries so that it can be referred to later on.

Teacher's notes

The shorter reading question pg 132–3

Objectives targeted TW**3**, 7

Starter

The focus of many previous NC Test reading questions has been on the writer's craft. The aim of the starter is to remind students of some of the technical language and devices that writers use to create an effect. Students should be able to include similes, metaphors, adjectival clauses and phrases, as well as adverbs, among their suggestions.

Display examples in the classroom to remind students of some of the terms they should be confident of using in the test. Remind them that it is important not just to identify these devices, but also to be able to comment on the effect they create on the reader.

Differentiation

If you think that some students may need some support, give them some of the terms and ask them to make up examples, or give them the examples and ask them to name what they are, or give them both as a mix and match exercise.

Introduction ws 104

This lesson should be used to explore ways of approaching the reading questions in the NC Test. In the following lesson these skills can be put into practice in a 'mock' test question under timed conditions. Give each student a copy of the extract and questions on **Worksheet 104**. Identifying the purpose, form and audience of a piece is a good starting point as it helps to put the writing into context, influencing other judgements that can be made about the piece. Make sure that students appreciate this point in the feedback session.

Development

Read through the 'Use your reading time effectively' box and ensure that students understand why it is necessary to follow this procedure in the test. Interaction with the text by highlighting is an important skill to encourage. Students should have enough time to plan their response and then finish it for homework, timing themselves to see what they can achieve when there are time constraints.

The longer reading question pg 134–5

Objectives targeted W4; TW**3**, 7

Starter ws 105

Time will be tight this lesson, if students are to complete the timed activities. The starter is designed to remind students about their word attack skills and to prepare them for some of the vocabulary they will face in the passage later on. Give each student a copy of **Worksheets 105a–b** so that they can use the context of the passage to work out the meaning of some of the words.

Introduction

Giving students time to read through the passage will help them to prepare for the real test, so it is important to remind them of how they should be using their time before they start. In later feedback, you could ask students to write their names on the question paper they are using so that you have an idea about who has followed the advice about interacting with the text – highlighting and annotating.

Development

As this is a practice, it would be useful to tell students when 10 minutes is up so that they know when they should be moving on to question 2.

Plenary

Use this part of the lesson to encourage students to reflect on their experience and think about what they need to do next time.

The writing question (1) pg 136–7

Objectives targeted W**3**, 4; TW**3**, 11

Starter

Correct spelling is important in the writing section of Paper 1, particularly if students are to achieve the higher levels. However, it is also important not to over-emphasize the point if it produces the reaction 'I'm no good at English because I can't spell' – an illusion that many students suffer from. Make sure that students bring their particular words to the next lesson, when they will be tested on them by their partner, or ask them to give you a copy of their words before they leave.

Teacher's notes

Differentiation

Very able spellers may find this task unnecessary, in which case they could be directed towards helping their more needy classmates, or spend their time widening their vocabulary through the use of a thesaurus. For example, 'How many different words can you find to describe the different shades of the primary colours?'

Introduction

If students have taken the optional tests in Years 7 and 8, then they will need to have it pointed out that in this test there is only **one** writing task, and that they have a choice. The task is more like the major writing task in the optional tests.

In the next lesson students will be given an opportunity to respond to a writing task within a time limit. The aim of this lesson is to examine a question in detail and explore some of the techniques that can be used to write well. Point out that the bullet points under the set task are important. They act as a guide to what should be covered, but do not need to be followed in the same order. It is wise to cover all the points as marks are allocated specifically for this purpose.

Development

Give each student a copy of **Worksheets 106** and **107**. The four opening paragraphs are essentially about the same experience, but approached in different ways by each writer. (See if students are aware of this after the feedback session.) The aim is to allow students the opportunity of discussing the different effect on the reader created through the writer's approach and style. You may like to use the jigsaw method, as described in the Teacher's Resources for Book 1, pages 43–4.

If you want to ask students to try giving the pieces a level, then copies of the NC level descriptors for writing would be useful. Note that the errors in the extracts are deliberate and should be taken into consideration when assessing the pieces, particularly the spelling in extract 4. Putting the paragraphs in order of merit might give rise to some interesting discussion among English teachers, let alone students. The following is a reliable guide:

Extract 3 'The best journey that I have ever made' (Level 4)
Extract 4 'Women pilots are few and far between' (Level 5)
Extract 1 'Have you ever seen the dawn' (Level 6)
Extract 2 'Dawn. Magical time of day.' (Level 7)

Differentiation

As an extension task for the quicker/more able students, ask them to:
- Comment on the technique that each writer has used in the opening sentences. Which are the most effective ways of capturing the reader's interest?
- Examine the variations of sentence length that the different writers have used. What effect do they create and what do they tell you about the skill of the writer concerned?
- Find three good points and one target for each extract.
- Determine what a level 8 piece of writing would look like. What would the writer of extract 2 have to do in order to achieve level 8?

Plenary

If written on paper, responses could also be used as classroom display to act as reminders.

The writing question (2) pg 138–9

Objectives targeted W3; TW3, 13

Time is very tight in this lesson – in fact it may be necessary, if you wish to give students the correct amount of time, to 'borrow' some time from the next lesson if this is feasible, or stretch into break/lunchtime.

Starter

It would help to reward students who have shown a marked improvement since the last lesson.

Introduction

Keeping to the time limit here should help to maintain the focus. Students will probably not have time to read everything, so ask them to concentrate on the opening paragraph, for example, putting into practice what they learnt in the previous lesson.

Development

Give each student a copy of the question paper (**Worksheet 108**). Read through the bullet points on the notice board before asking students to start. Remind them that in the test they will probably have three choices, but in this case they have already written on one of the choices in the previous lesson.

Differentiation

Some students may benefit from a writing frame,

Teacher's notes

but as these are not available in the test itself, it may give rise to false expectations.

Plenary

If appropriate, for homework, students could be asked to write a response to the final task that they have not chosen. It would then be useful to see what type of writing they actually do best, and they may be surprised at the results.

The Shakespeare paper (1) pg 140–41

Objectives targeted TR14; TW3

The Shakespeare paper at the end of KS3, for most students, will be the first time that they will be taking a literature test on a set text. The notion of knowing a text thoroughly, including being able to find key quotations to illustrate their points, is one that needs to be stressed in the preparation period leading up to the test itself.

In keeping with the earlier 'Inform, explain, describe' section, these next two lessons focus on the play of *Macbeth*. However, if your class has been studying one of the other two plays, you could follow the same pattern of work, substituting questions on your chosen text in the place of those on *Macbeth*.

Starter (ws 109)

Give a copy of **Worksheet 109** to each student. If you want, you could try dividing the class into two teams, awarding points and bonus points, or base the quiz on one of the popular TV quiz shows. The central aim, whatever form of delivery you choose, is to stress the importance of a sound knowledge of the text studied.

Introduction (ws 110)

Give a copy of **Worksheet 110** to each student. A good deal of information and helpful hints is given in this section. It may be an idea to vary the delivery by asking different students to read parts out loud, or to make comments on the advice given. Leave plenty of time for the feedback session to emphasize important points about the questions and the nature of the responses required.

Development

Use the planning stage as an opportunity to emphasize to students that planning, including making sure that the bullet points have been covered, is very important. Encourage the practice of using highlighters again to highlight key points on the question paper.

The Shakespeare paper (2) pg 142–3

Objectives targeted TR14; TW3

If you want, this practice paper to be just like the real thing, you may wish to consider copying the appropriate scenes so that students can have plain texts to refer to, as they do in the actual test. The text of all Shakespeare's plays can be found on the internet.

As Paper 2 is actually longer than most English lessons, 1 hour 15 minutes, you may wish to plan ahead for this exercise by 'borrowing' time from another lesson, if this is feasible

Starter

Secure understanding of these key words is essential if students are to express their ideas with clarity in the test. If you wish, the task could be made into a quick 'warm up' quiz.

Introduction and development (ws 111)

Give a copy of **Worksheet 111** to each student. You may find it helpful, if time is tight, to go through the 'Top tips' on page 143 in an earlier lesson. Guiding students through the time planning at this stage may help them to understand how time needs to be spread and used effectively. Otherwise the single task on this fairly long paper may appear rather daunting.

Differentiation

Students on levels 3 to 4 may find it useful to have the support of the 'Top tip' during the test, or an accompanying writing frame. However, it would need to be clearly explained that these will not be allowed in the actual test.

GCSE English pg 144–5

These last three lessons are designed for the end of the summer term, to help prepare students for their GCSE course in Years 10 and 11. They include some explanation of what the course will contain, as well as elements of self-assessment and target setting.

Starter

This is an opportunity for teachers and students to celebrate and reflect upon what has been learnt and enjoyed during Key Stage 3. A sense of achievement is to be encouraged in order to

Teacher's notes

inspire students to develop skills still further in the coming years.

Introduction [ws 112]

When talking through the GCSE outline on **Worksheet 112**, explain the particular information that applies to the GCSE course and examinations that the students in your school will be taking.

Development

One of the main differences between assessment at GCSE and Key Stage 3 are the coursework and speaking and listening elements, which only appear as part of the teacher assessment in KS3. Stress the importance of these through the activity.

GCSE English Literature [pg 146-7]

Objectives targeted TR13

Most students nowadays take both English and English Literature at GCSE, but even if some of your students will not be taking literature, you may still wish to use this lesson. English contains a fair degree of literature in the coursework element. The reading challenge for the summer holidays would be appropriate for all. You may wish to relate this challenge to the National Reading Challenge Plus. Contact your local library for details.

It would be useful to hold this lesson in the library where students can be introduced to books for the development activity, or browse and make choices of their own.

Starter

It is astonishing how many students take GCSE English Literature every year without really understanding what it means (or even being able to spell the word correctly). This activity aims to help them appreciate the meaning of the term and realize that they have already studied a good deal of literature.

Introduction [ws 113]

The reading self-evaluation (**Worksheet 113**), when completed independently, could be used later as a starting point for discussion, perhaps at the beginning of Year 10, or as the basis for pair/groupwork discussion.

Development [ws 114]

Give each student a copy of the reading statement on **Worksheet 114**. Setting challenging reading targets is important at this stage, but each student will have a different area that needs developing. Maintaining a balance between non-fiction and fiction is a sensible idea, as is the need to try to distinguish between literature and 'reading books' of the horror/thriller/crime/romance variety.

If the lesson is being held in the library, allow some time for students to browse and make their own choices. The teacher and librarian can then offer assistance to ensure that appropriate choices have been made.

Self-evaluation [pg 148-9]

Objectives targeted TR1, 5, 13; TW1

Starter [ws 115]

Give each student a copy of **Worksheet 115**. Understanding SMART targets is central to the business of setting future goals. They have been used before in the *English Frameworking* series, so students should be familiar with the concept.

Introduction [ws 116]

The reading skills self-evaluation (**Worksheet 116**) is not directly linked to NC levels, although the range is clearly derived from it. Students are not being asked to give themselves a level at this stage. It is more a question of appreciating the skills that they have developed and reflecting on which skills they could sensibly improve upon.

Development [ws 117]

As with the reading evaluation, the writing evaluation (**Worksheet 117**) looks at range and style. Note the words of advice in the box on page 149, so that students do not set themselves up for instant failure by being too hard on themselves (as they often are).

You may like to arrange for the Year 10 English teachers of the individual students to have a copy of both self-evaluation sheets. They are a valuable student profile resource, and enable targets to be followed through and taken further.

Reviewing Year 8: Looking forward to Year 9

Worksheet 1

What do you read?

pg 7

Name:
Form:

Highlight any sections that describe what you read and give some examples of the sort of texts you have read within these sections.

Fiction					
Novels and short stories	horror stories	science fiction	detective/ mystery	romance	classics/ all-time greats
	historical/war	fantasy	adventure	natural world	other
Fact					
	autobiography	biography	sport	natural world	travel writing
	hobbies	diaries/letters	manuals	other	other
Magazines	sport	hobbies	fashion and romance	music	other
Newspapers	news	sport	stars	television	other
Internet (state which areas)					
Other					

English Frameworking 3: Teacher's Resources © HarperCollins Publishers 2002

Reviewing Year 8: Looking forward to Year 9 — Worksheet 2

Evaluating your reading skills

Name:
Form:

Fill in the grid below.

Focus	Can do confidently	Can do sometimes	Have difficulty with	What I need to do to improve in this area
Describe, select or retrieve information, events or ideas from text and use quotation and reference to text				
Deduce, infer or interpret information, events or ideas from text				
Comment on the structure and organization of texts, including grammatical and presentational features				
Comment on writers' use of language including grammatical and literary features				
Comment on writers' purposes and viewpoints and the effect of the text on the reader				

Look at the reading skills targets that you set yourself at the end of last year. Decide if they are still appropriate and amend them if necessary:

- ....
- ....
- ....

Now reflect on your reading preferences and decide on two or three targets to expand the range of texts that you read:

- ....
- ....
- ....

English Frameworking 3: Teacher's Resources © HarperCollinsPublishers 2002

Reviewing Year 8: Looking forward to Year 9 — Worksheet 3

The ingredients of text

Typical ingredients	diagrams	use of visual image to attract attention
Not typical ingredients	evaluation	list of materials/ equipment
?	bias	flowcharts
chronological	introduction	characterization
logical order	emotive language	bullet points
imperative	temporal connectives	dialogue
colloquial	concise	impersonal
past tense	omniscient author	retells events
formal	Standard English	describes the way things are
1st person	figurative language	use of rhetorical devices
quotation	3rd person	subordinate clause
analysis	present tense	explains processes involved or how things work
2nd person	causal connectives	promotes a particular view or event
autobiographical style	conclusion	presents arguments from different viewpoints

Reviewing Year 8: Looking forward to Year 9

Worksheet 4a

Examples of text types (1)

We came from Bethlehem, Georgia, bearing Betty Crocker cake mixes into the jungle. My sisters and I were all counting on having one birthday apiece during our twelve-month mission. 'And heaven knows,' our mother predicted, 'they won't have Betty Crocker in the Congo.'

'Where we are headed, there will *be* no buyers and sellers at all,' my father corrected. His tone implied that mother failed to grasp our mission, and that her concern with Betty Crocker confederated her with the coin-jingling sinners who vexed Jesus till he pitched a fit and threw them out of church. 'Where we are headed,' he said, to make things perfectly clear, 'not so much as a Piggly Wiggly.' Evidently father saw this as a point in the Congo's favour. I got the most spectacular chills, just from trying to imagine.

She wouldn't go against him, of course. But once she understood there was no turning back, our mother went to laying out in the spare bedroom all the worldly things she thought we'd need in the Congo just to scrape by. 'The bare minimum, for my children,' she'd declare under her breath, all the livelong day ...

Narrative: Opening paragraphs of *The Poisonwood Bible* by Barbara Kingsolver

Block diagrams

Action planning requires you to be logical. You must work out what needs to be done and in what order. The simplest way to make a plan is in a block diagram. Write down all the tasks that need to be done, then put them in order. Draw a box around each task. You may be able to group related tasks together in one box. The boxes show the stages in the making process. Link these together with arrows. Fig. 1.52 shows a block diagram for making an apple crumble. Use the method listed in your recipe to work out all the stages you will need to complete.

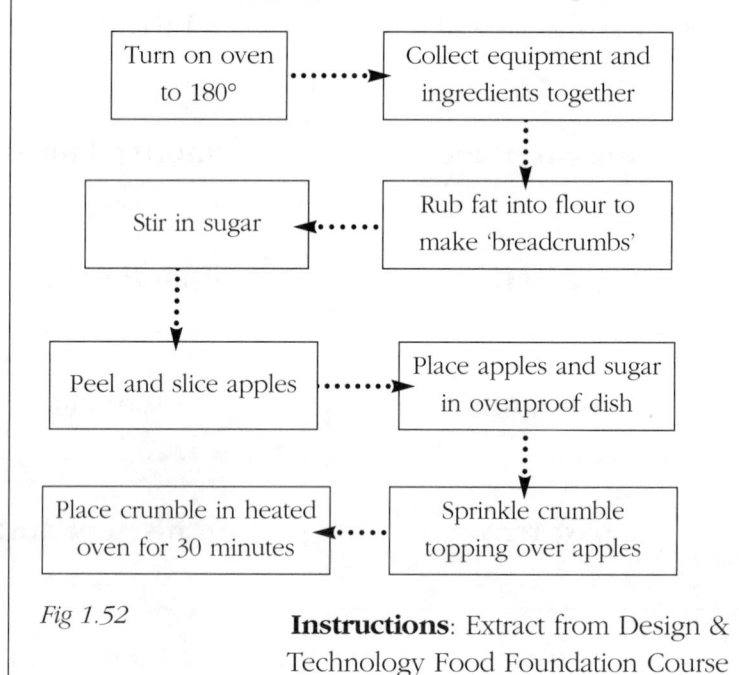

```
Turn on oven        →   Collect equipment and
to 180°                 ingredients together
                              ↓
Stir in sugar       ←   Rub fat into flour to
                        make 'breadcrumbs'
    ↓
Peel and slice apples →  Place apples and sugar
                         in ovenproof dish
                              ↓
Place crumble in heated ←  Sprinkle crumble
oven for 30 minutes        topping over apples
```

Fig 1.52

Instructions: Extract from Design & Technology Food Foundation Course

---

I have a dream that one day even the state of Mississippi, a desert state, sweltering with the heat of injustice and oppression, will be transformed into an oasis of freedom and justice.
I have a dream that my four children will one day live in a nation where they will not be judged by the color of their skin but by the content of their character.
I have a dream today.
I have a dream that one day the state of Alabama, whose governor's lips are presently dripping with the words of <u>interposition and nullification</u>,[1] will be transformed into a situation where little black boys and black girls will be able to join hands with little white boys and white girls and walk together as sisters and brothers.
I have a dream today.
I have a dream that one day every valley shall be <u>exalted</u>,[2] every hill and mountain shall be made low, the rough places will be made plain, and the crooked places will be made straight, and the glory of the Lord shall be revealed, and all flesh shall see it together.

Persuasion: Extract from Martin Luther's speech in Washington DC, 28 August 1963

[1] *being obstructive and negative*   [2] *raised high*

Examples of text types (2)

Thirty years after the Second World War had ended, an especially thoughtful airman said to me, 'Never forget war is about destroying things and killing people.' The triumph of 1940, the heroism of the Royal Airforce pilots, the bravery of the civilian population beneath the bombers of the Luftwaffe[1] was real, remarkable and should never be forgotten. The images that keep the memory alive are from the celluloid of contemporary newsreel and retrospective reconstruction for the cinema – the exquisite shape of a Spitfire coming, as if out of the sun, to destroy wave after wave of German aircraft with its Browning guns ablaze; of old ladies being hauled out of a ruined street in the East End peering at the cinema and declaring in perfect Cockney that 'one day, that 'itler, 'e'll go too far.'

But the image which haunts me most is that of the basket of 'unidentified flesh' the wardens were instructed to gather from the rubble after a raid for use in the mortuaries where attendants spent long hours putting together something resembling a body for distraught[2] relatives to bury. It's an image which anyone of a later generation that did not live through the Blitz[3] needs to keep vivid …

Recount: Extract from *Never Again: Britain 1945–1951* by Peter Hennessey

[1] *German airforce* [2] *upset*
[3] *systematic bombing of Britain in 1940–41 by the Luftwaffe*

The great American muck-raking journalist, I. F. Stone, wrote: 'Every government is run by liars, and nothing they say should be believed.' He exaggerated, though not much; governments are the prime source of propaganda,[1] of which lying by degree is of essence. When the First World War was over, Philip Gibbs, the British correspondent, reflected: 'Some of us wrote the truth from the first to the last, apart from the naked realism of horrors and losses and criticisms of facts, *which did not come within the liberty of our pen.*' The italics are mine; the rare honesty is his. In the 1980s, with nuclear war a real prospect, the spreading of 'our propaganda' by journalists is no less common than it was in Gibbs' time, perhaps more so. The difference is that there was a public agonising by journalists; today there is silence.

Since the Second World War, which was generally reported as simply a great crusade, as our good guys against their bad guys, war has not fallen into disgrace as some would wish to believe, and certainly not in the media: witness the born-again front page jingoism[2] during the Falklands episode[3] …

Discursive: Preface to *Nukespeak: The Media and the Bomb* by John Pilger

[1] *organized programme of publicity*
[2] *aggressive patriotism*
[3] *Britain's war with Argentina over the Falkland Islands in 1982*

The following 12 pages present a chronological synopsis[1] of the major events in world history. The entries, necessarily abbreviated, are set out in columns under regional headings which vary from period to period according to shifts in historical geography. A separate column lists important cultural events (in the broadest sense including not only music art and literature but also science and technology) in all regions of the world. Together with the glossary and with the geographical index, page 335, the Chronology provides a key to the individual plates and maps, designed to help the reader to place the events narrated there in the broader context of world history. It also indicates (in bold type) the key events in different regions, at different times, and the specific contributions of each to the development of civilization and of civilized life. The calendar of events starts with the beginnings of agriculture around the year 9000 BC. For a time-scale of prehistory refer to the time chart on page 36.

Explanation: Extract from *The Times Atlas of World History*, 1993

[1] *summary*

Laws can be divided into two types. Laws about crimes, such as theft, vandalism and assault, which the government enforces, are part of what is called **criminal law**. Laws concerning your private rights in your dealings with other people, such as borrowing and lending money, are part of what is called **civil law**.

There are also two systems of law courts. **Criminal courts** deal with people accused of criminal offences. About 98% of criminal cases are dealt with in **magistrates' courts**. Serious offences are dealt with in **crown courts**, before a judge and a jury.

Civic cases are dealt with in **civil courts**. Minor cases are dealt with in courts called **county courts**, and important cases are dealt with in the **High Court**.

England and Wales have the same system of laws and law courts. But Scotland and Northern Ireland have their own separate systems.

Information: Extract from *Your Life: The Complete Course for PHSE and Citizenship* by John Foster

Reviewing Year 8: Looking forward to Year 9

Worksheet 5

Reviewing your writing skills

pg 9

Name:
Form:

Fill in the following grid, indicating which areas of your writing you feel confident about and which need to be improved. Then decide on your three most immediate writing targets.

Text type or skill		Feel confident about	Needs improving
Fiction	Narrative and creative writing		
	Poetry		
	Playscripts		
Non-fiction	Instructions		
	Advice		
	Information		
	Recount		
	Persuasion		
	Explanation		
	Discursive • Analysis		
	• Evaluation		
	• Formal essay		
Structure	Planning: Is my writing clearly structured and appropriate to the logic of the topic?		
	Introductions: Do I write effective introductions that set the direction of the writing and interest the reader?		
	Paragraphing: Can I handle paragraphs in a wide range of writing, indicating a change in topic or direction?		
	Connectives: Do I link my ideas effectively in a variety of ways?		
Grammar and punctuation	Punctuation: Do I use the key forms of punctuation effectively to help the reader understand my ideas? Grammar: Is the structuring of my sentences grammatically sound?		
Style	Do I use a variety of sentence structures and vocabulary effectively?		
Spelling	Is my spelling of all widely used vocabulary including complex words secure?		
Handwriting	Is my handwriting legible and sustainable under pressure?		

Writing targets for the coming half term:
- _____
- _____
- _____

46

English Frameworking 3: Teacher's Resources © HarperCollinsPublishers 2002

Reviewing Year 8: Looking forward to Year 9 — Worksheet 6

Vocabulary related to geometry

Link: begin with tri (contain 3 of something)	kite	square	triple
Link: all contain angles	triangle	reflex	hexagon
Link: are all types of angle	sides	equilateral	obtuse
Link: are all types of triangle	parallelogram	trisect	right angled
Link: a triangle has 3	acute	rhombus	triplets
vertices (vertex)	angle(s)	right	trapezium
rectangle	tripod	isosceles	scalene

Reviewing Year 8: Looking forward to Year 9

Worksheet 7

Key terms from across the curriculum

D&T	Science	PE	History	Art	Geography
carbohydrate	absorb	accuracy	bias	abstract	amenities
component	acid	activity	chronology	atmosphere	climate
criteria	alkaline	agility	civilization	collage	country
design brief	apparatus	athletic	conflict	colour	economy
disassemble	chemical	bicep	constitution	composition	employment
evaluation	circulation	control	current	contrast	environment
fabric	combustion	exercise	defence	crosshatch	erosion
fibre	condensation	field	document	design	estuary
flowchart	digestion	gymnastic	economy	dimension	infrastructure
ingredient	dissolve	hamstring	evidence	expressionist	international
innovation	distil	injury	government	foreground	landscape
machine	element	league	imperialism	frieze	latitude
manufacture	evaporation	medicine	independence	highlight	longitude
natural	experiment	mobility	invasion	influence	meteorology
nutrition	friction	movement	motive	impressionist	physical
research	liquid	muscle	parliament	landscape	pollution
portfolio	method	pitch	political	observation	regional
presentation	nutrient	position	propaganda	perspective	resources
production	organism	quadriceps	rebellion	portrait	rural
proposal	oxygen	qualify	reign	primitive	settlement
protein	particle	relay	religious	realist	tourism
recipe	reproduce	squad	republic	romantic	transportation
specification	respiration	tactic	revolution	technique	urban
tension	solution	tournament	siege	texture	wealth
textile	temperature	triceps	source	tone	weather

English Frameworking 3: Teacher's Resources © HarperCollinsPublishers 2002

Reviewing Year 8: Looking forward to Year 9

Worksheet 8

Key weaknesses in the alibis

Name:
Form:

Use the grid below to note down all the evidence that you think breaks the alibi, in order of importance. Justify your selection by adding a comment in the right-hand column.

Alibi 1

Key weaknesses in alibi	Why significant?
1	
2	
3	
4	
5	

Alibi 2

Key weaknesses in alibi	Why significant?
1	
2	
3	
4	
5	

Advice to alibi group:
-
-
-

Advice to cross-questioners:
-
-
-

Reviewing Year 8: Looking forward to Year 9 — **Worksheet 9**

Sentence starters for Alibis essay

The purpose of the game Alibis is …

By the end of the cross-examination the prosecution decided that …

The group that I have selected to illustrate the game is … because …

The key evidence to support this decision was …

To begin the game, the alibi group (the suspects) goes outside the classroom and …

By the end of this case, the class had learnt that in order to construct a successful alibi it is necessary to …

During this time, the rest of the class (the prosecution) discuss …

The class also learnt that …

Through interviewing the first suspect, the prosecution established that …

In conclusion, Alibis is a good game to play because …

Possible weaknesses to follow up with the next suspect were …

'This Fella I Knew' by Bernard MacLaverty

This fella I knew – he spent his boyhood in a place between here and Sleivemish – out beyond the point there. On the outskirts of Lettermacaward.

And wait till I tell you this. He earned the best part of fifty pounds a day folding shirts.

And the best part of it was, he never folded a shirt in his life. His mother said he just threw them at his backside. But he was smart enough for being rared on a bit of a farm.

And he went to the University in Belfast. And did a degree in all kinds of things – engineering and physics and mathy-matics and God knows what.

And at the finish-up didn't he get a job across the water folding shirts. In a big concern. Marks and Spencer's, I think it was.

A new shirt, now, is an experience. And, before our friend with his University degrees got on the job, it was a dangerous one – for you could end up going out till a dance needing a blood transfusion, there was that many stabs in you from putting on the new shirt. That was until our friend came along – with the mathy-matics and the engineering. Folding, it seems, is a science. I'm told a bit of paper can't be folded more than eight times, no matter should it be a sheet the size of Ireland itself. Anyway, the aim of the thing was to get the shirt folding down to the one pin. And this your man did – no bother.

And they paid him a powerful sum of money for the knack of doing this.

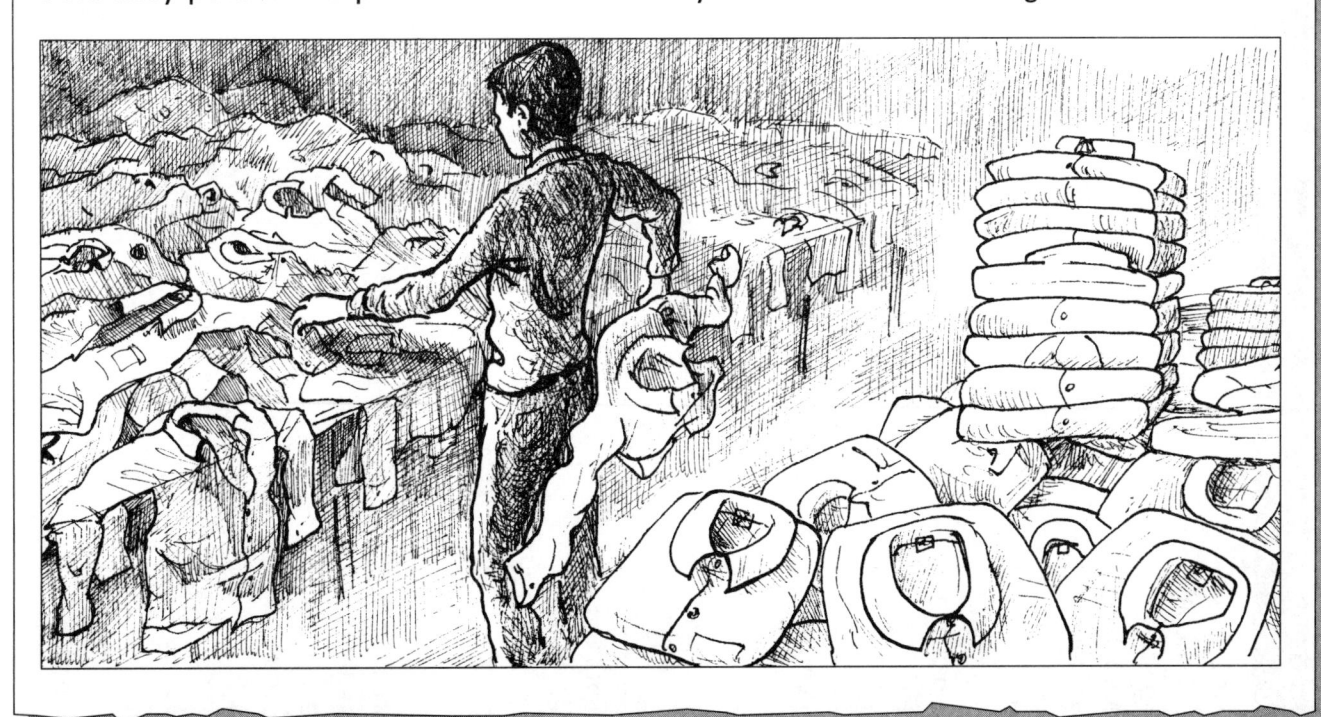

Imagine, explore, entertain: Writers from various cultures

Worksheet 11

Analysing 'This Fella I Knew'

pg 19

Name:
Form:

Question	Point	Evidence	Comment
1 Why do you think the author chose to tell this story in the persona of the storyteller?			
2 What sort of lifestyle do you think the narrator is used to?			
3 What do you learn about Northern Irish cultural traditions from this story?			
4 What does the storyteller think about the mother in the story?			
5 Which phrases or sentences that the writer has used do you think are most effective?			
6 What features make this story entertaining?			

Imagine, explore, entertain: Writers from various cultures — Worksheet 12

Word origins (pg 20)

sputnik	**butcher's** (meaning look)	**fiancé**
wicked (meaning very good)	**dialect**	**potato**
tattoo	**bungalow**	**fort**
macho		**French**
Greek	**Spanish**	**Hindi**
Latin	**Russian**	**Cockney rhyming slang**
American slang	**Spanish**	**Dutch**

English Frameworking 3: Teacher's Resources   © HarperCollinsPublishers 2002

Imagine, explore, entertain: Writers from various cultures

'A Woman of No Standing' (cont.) by Brendan Behan

Worksheet 13

He was still alive when I got down to the Pigeon House but she wasn't far out because he didn't last out the night.

His face all caved in, and his hair that was once so brown and curly was matted in sweat, and God knows what colour.

Ah, you'd pity him all right, for the ruined remains of what was once the gassest[1] little ex-Dublin Fusilier in the street – off with the belt and who began it – Up the Toughs, Throttle the Turks, and Hell blast Gallipoli.[2]

Ria, his wife, was the kindest woman in Ireland, and (I've heard my mother say) in her day, the best looking.

He died that night and the nun and Ria and Máire were charmed that he'd no mortal sin on his soul to detain him in torment for any longer than a few short years of harmonious torture in Purgatory.[3]

The priest was delighted too, because, as he said: 'It's not when you die, but how you die that matters.'

As for the woman, no one saw her to know what she thought of it, but the priest gave strict orders that she wasn't to be let near the funeral.

The funeral was on the day after. He'd lain the night before in the mortuary chapel. They've a mortuary chapel in the Pigeon House sanatorium, nice and handy, and most soothing, I'm sure, to new patients coming in, it being close by the entrance gate.

There used to be an old scribble on the porch that said: 'Let all who enter here, leave hope behind.' But some hard chaw[4] had the beatings of that and wrote: 'It's only a step from Killarney to heaven – come here and take the lift – any lung, chum?'

We had a few prayers that night, but she never turned up, and I was sorry, because to tell the truth, I was curious to see her.

At the funeral next day, our cars (Ria did it in style all right, whatever lingering scald her heart hold for him) greased off the wet Pigeon House Road, through Ringsend, and into Pearse Street, and still no sign of her. Right up the Northside, and all the way to Glasnevin, and she never appeared.

Ria had the hearse go round the block where we'd all lived years ago – happy, healthy, though riotous betimes – fighting being better than loneliness.

I thought she'd have ambushed us here, but she didn't.

I had some idea of a big car (owned by a new and tolerant admirer) sweeping into the cortege from some side street or another, or else a cab that'd slide in, a woman in rich mourning heavily veiled in its corner.

But between the Pigeon House and the grave not a one came near us.

The sods were thrown in and all, and the grave diggers well away to it when Máire spotted her.

'Mother, get the full of your eyes of that one.'

'Where, alanna?'[5] asks Ria.

'There,' said Máire, pointing to a tree behind us. I looked towards it.

All I could see was a poor middle-aged woman, bent in haggard prayer, dressed in the cast-off hat and coat of some flahool[6] old one she'd been doing a day's work for (maybe not so flahool either, for sometimes they'll stop a day's pay on the head of some old rag, rejected from a jumble sale).

'But I thought,' says I to Ria, 'that she'd be like – like – that she'd be dolled up to the nines – paint and powder and a fur coat maybe.'

'Fur coat how are you!' said Ria scornfully, 'and she out scrubbing halls for me dear departed this last four years – since he took bad.'

She went off from behind her tree before we left the cemetery.

When Ria, Máire and myself got into The Brian Boru, there she was at the end of the counter.

I called two drinks and a mineral for Máire, and as soon as she heard my voice, she looked up, finished her gill of plain porter and went off.

She passed quite near us and she going out the door – her head down and a pale hunted look in her eyes.

---

[1] Dublin slang for fun   [2] site of major battle in Turkey in the First World War   [3] a place where souls are purified from sin   [4] an uncouth rustic   [5] an affectionate term for a child, from the gaelic a leanbh   [6] generous, lavish, from the Gaelic flaithiuil

Imagine, explore, entertain: Writers from various cultures — **Worksheet 14a**

'Stench of Kerosene' by Amrita Pritam (1)

Name
Form

Outside, a mare neighed. Guleri recognised the neighing and ran out of the house. The mare was from her parents' village. She put her head against its neck as if it were the door to her father's house.

Guleri's parents lived in Chamba. A few miles from her husband's village which was on high ground, the road curved and descended steeply downhill. From this point one could see Chamba lying a long way away at one's feet. Whenever Guleri was homesick she would take her husband, Manak, and go up to this point. She would see the homes of Chamba twinkling in the sunlight and would come back, her heart glowing with pride.

Once every year, after the harvest had been gathered in, Guleri was allowed to spend a few days with her parents. They sent a man to Lakarmandi to bring her back to Chamba. Two of her friends, who were also married to boys who lived away from Chamba, came home at the same time and the girls looked forward to their annual reunion, talking about their joys and sorrow. They went about the streets together. Then there was the harvest festival when the girls would have new clothes made for the occasion. Their dupattas[1] would be dyed, starched and sprinkled with mica[2] to make them glisten. They would buy glass bangles and silver ear-rings.

Guleri always counted the days to the harvest. When autumn breezes cleared the skies of monsoon clouds, she thought of little else. She went about her daily chores – fed the cattle, cooked food for her parents-in-law – and then sat back to work out how long it would be before someone came to fetch her from her parent's village.

And now, once again, it was time for her annual visit. She caressed the mare joyfully, greeted her father's servant, Natu, and made preparations to leave the next day. She did not have to express her excitement in words: the look on her face was enough. Her husband pulled at his hookah[3] and closed his eyes. It seemed as if he either did not like the tobacco or that he could not bear to face his wife.

'You'll come to the fair at Chamba, won't you? Come even for a day,' she pleaded.

Manak put aside his chillum[4] but did not reply. 'Why don't you answer me?' she asked, a little cross. 'Shall I tell you something?'

'I know what you're going to say – that you only go to your parents once a year. Well you've never been stopped before.'

'Then why do you want to stop me this time?' she demanded.

'Just this once,' he pleaded.

'Your mother's said nothing so why do you stand in the way?' Guleri was childishly stubborn.

'My mother …' Manak did not finish his sentence.

On the long-awaited morning, Guleri was ready long before dawn. She had no children and therefore no problem of having to leave them behind or take them with her. Natu saddled the mare as she took leave of Manak's parents. They patted her head and blessed her.

'I'll come with you for part of the way,' Manak said.

Guleri was happy as they set out. She hid Manak's flute under her dupatta.

After the village of Khajiar, the road descended steeply to Chamba. There she took out the flute and gave it to him. She took his hand in hers and said, 'Come now, play your flute.' But Manak, lost in his thoughts, paid no heed. 'Why don't you play your flute?' she asked, coaxing him. He looked at her sadly. Then putting the flute to his lips, blew a strange anguished wail.

'Guleri, don't go away,' he begged her. 'I ask again, don't go away this time.' He handed the flute to her, unable to continue.

'But why?' she asked. 'Come over on the day of the fair and we'll return together, I promise you.'

Manak did not ask again.

---

[1] *a piece of cloth worn over a blouse like a stole* [2] *a mineral of different colours* [3] *a tobacco pipe*
[4] *a small clay pipe for smoking tobacco*

Imagine, explore, entertain: Writers from various cultures — Worksheet 14b

'Stench of Kerosene' by Amrita Pritam (2)

They stopped by the roadside. Natu took the mare a few paces ahead to leave the couple alone. It crossed Manak's mind that it was at this time of the year, seven years ago, that he and his friends had come on this very road to go to the harvest festival in Chamba. And it was at this fair that Manak had first seen Guleri and they had bartered their hearts to each other. Later, managing to meet her alone, he remembered taking her hand and telling her, 'You are like unripe corn – full of milk.'

'Cattle go for unripe corn,' Guleri had replied, freeing her hand with a jerk. 'Human beings prefer it roasted. If you want me, go and ask my father for my hand.'

Among Manak's kinsmen it was customary to settle the bride price[1] before the wedding. Manak was nervous because he did not know the price Guleri's father would demand from him. But Guleri's father was prosperous and had lived in cities. He had sworn that he would not take money for his daughter but would give her to a worthy young man from a good family. Manak, he decided, answered these requirements and soon after, Guleri and Manak were married. Deep in memories, Manak was roused by Guleri's hand on his shoulder.

'What are you dreaming of?' she teased him.

He did not answer. The mare neighed impatiently and Guleri got up to leave. 'Do you know the bluebell wood a couple of miles from here?' she asked. 'It's said that anyone who goes through it becomes deaf. You must have passed through that bluebell wood. You don't seem to be hearing anything I say.'

'You're right, Guleri. I can't hear anything you're saying to me,' and Manak sighed.

They looked at each other. Neither understood the other's thoughts. 'I'll go now,' Guleri said gently. 'You'd better go back. You've come a long way from home.'

'You've walked all the distance. You'd better get on the mare,' replied Manak.

'Here, take your flute.'

'You take it.'

'Will you come and play it on the day of the fair?' she asked with a smile. The sun shone in her eyes. Manak turned his face away. Perplexed, Guleri shrugged her shoulders and took the road to Chamba. Manak returned home.

He entered the house and slumped listlessly on the charpoy.[2] 'You've been away a long time,' exclaimed his mother. 'Did you go all the way to Chamba?'

'Not all the way, only to the top of the hill.' Manak's voice was heavy.

'Why do you croak like an old woman?' said his mother severely. 'Be a man.'

Manak wanted to retort, 'You are a woman; why don't you cry like one for a change!' But he remained silent.

Manak and Guleri had been married seven years but she had never borne a child and Manak's mother had made a secret resolve that she would not let it go beyond the eighth year. This year, true to her decision, she had paid five hundred rupees[3] to get him a second wife and she was waiting, as Manak knew, for Guleri to go to her parents before bringing in the new bride. Obedient to his mother and to custom, Manak's body responded to the new woman but his heart was dead within him.

In the early hours one morning he was smoking his chillum when an old friend happened to pass by. 'Ho, Bhavani, where are you going so early in the morning?'

Bhavani stopped. He had a small bundle on his shoulder. 'Nowhere in particular,' he said evasively.

'You should be on your way to some place or the other,' exclaimed Manak. 'What about a smoke?'

---

[1] a price paid to a bride's family by the bridegroom   [2] a wooden bed strung with rope   [3] Indian currency

Imagine, explore, entertain: Writers from various cultures — Worksheet **14c**

'Stench of Kerosene' by Amrita Pritam (3)

Bhavani sat down on his haunches and took the chillum from Manak's hands. 'I'm going to Chamba for the fair,' he said at last.

Bhavani's words pierced through Manak's heart like a needle.

'Is the fair today?'

'It's the same day, every year,' replied Bhavani drily. 'Don't you remember, we were in the same party seven years ago?' Bhavani did not say any more but Manak was conscious of the other man's rebuke and he felt uneasy. Bhavani put down the chillum and picked up his bundle. His flute was sticking out of the bundle. Manak's eye remained on the flute till Bhavani disappeared from view.

Next morning, Manak was in his fields when he saw Bhavani coming back but he looked the other way deliberately. He did not want to talk to Bhavani to hear anything about the fair. But Bhavani came round the other side and sat down in front of Manak. His face was sad and grey as a cinder.

'Guleri is dead,' Bhavani said in a flat voice.

'What?'

'When she heard of your second marriage, she soaked her clothes in kerosene[1] and set fire to them.'

Manak, mute with pain, could only stare and feel his own life burning out.

The days went by. Manak resumed his work in the fields and ate his meals when they were given to him. But he was like a dead man, his face blank, his eyes empty.

'I am not his wife,' complained his second wife. 'I'm just someone he happened to marry.'

But quite soon she was pregnant and Manak's mother was pleased with her new daughter-in-law. She told Manak about his wife's condition, but he looked as if he did not understand and his eyes were still empty.

His mother encouraged her daughter-in-law to bear with her husband's moods for a few days. As soon as the child was born and placed in his father's lap, she said, Manak would change.

A son was duly born to Manak's wife; and his mother, rejoicing, bathed the boy, dressed him in fine clothes and put him in Manak's lap. Manak stared at the newborn babe in his lap. He stared a long time, uncomprehending, his face as usual expressionless. Then suddenly the blank eyes filled with horror and Manak began to scream. 'Take him away!' he shrieked hysterically, 'Take him away! He stinks of kerosene.'

[1] *paraffin*

Amrita Pritam was born in the Punjab in India in 1919 and is a leading Indian poet, often writing about traditional Punjabi folk heroes. In her fiction she has focused on many aspects of love.

Imagine, explore, entertain: Writers from various cultures — Worksheet 15

'Stench of Kerosene' – structure cards

The mare from Guleri's parents' village arrives at her house.	Background information establishing where Guleri's parents live and that Guleri and some friends have an annual reunion at her parents' village which she looks forward to.	Guleri is excited at the prospect of the journey to her old village but senses that this year her husband, Manak, does not want her to go.
Guleri sets out on the journey. Manak accompanies her for a short way and begs her not to go but does not explain why. He is unwilling to play his flute when she asks him to.	The reader is shown the thoughts inside Manak's head as he remembers his first meeting with his wife at the Chamba fair and their marriage.	Guleri interrupts Manak's thoughts but feels that her husband is not listening to her. She offers him the flute but he asks her to take it.
Manak returns home. His mother cross-questions him.	Background information telling the reader that Guleri and Manak are childless after seven years of marriage. Manak's mother has decided to pay for a second wife for her son.	Manak unwillingly goes along with his mother's plan.
Manak asks Bhavani, a friend who is passing, where he is going. Bhavani rebukes him for forgetting the Chamba fair.	Manak remembers how Bhavani was one of the group of friends with Manak when he first met Guleri at the fair seven years ago.	Manak is aware his friend is angry with him. Manak notices his friend is carrying a flute.
When Manak sees his friend returning from the fair, he tries to avoid him.	Bhavani tells Manak that Guleri has killed herself by soaking her clothes in kerosene and setting fire to them.	Manak's new wife is unhappy that Manak does not see her as his wife.
Manak's new wife becomes pregnant. Manak's mother is very pleased but Manak shows no interest.	Manak's mother assures the new wife that Manak will change once the child is born.	When the child is born, Manak rejects him. He associates him with kerosene.

Imagine, explore, entertain: Writers from various cultures — Worksheet 16

'Stench of Kerosene' – significant points

1 The story is positive up until this point.

2 The reader now understands why the Chamba fair is significant to both husband and wife.

3 The reader now understands that Guleri and Manak cannot communicate, though the reader does not, as yet, know why.

4 The reader realizes that Manak will not oppose his mother even though he wants to.

5 The reader first understands why Manak is so upset.

6 The reader realizes how strong Manak's sense of guilt is at deserting the wife whom he loves.

7 The reader is now certain that the baby will not reconcile Manak to his new wife.

Imagine, explore, entertain: Writers from various cultures — Worksheet 17a

'The Welcome Table' (cont.) by Alice Walker (1)

Name
Form

2. She was angular and lean and the color of poor gray Georgia earth, beaten by king cotton and the extreme weather. Her elbows were wrinkled and thick, the skin ashen but durable, like the bark of old pines. On her face centuries were folded into the circles around one eye, while around the other, etched and mapped as if for print, ages more threatened again to live. Some of them there at the church saw the age, the dotage, the missing buttons down the front of her mildewed black dress. Others saw cooks, chauffeurs, maids, mistresses, children denied or smothered in the deferential[1] way she held her cheek to one side, toward the ground. Many of them saw jungle orgies in an evil place, while others were reminded of riotous anarchists looting and raping in the streets. Those who knew the hesitant creeping up on them of the law, saw the beginning of the end of the sanctuary of Christian worship, saw the desecration[2] of Holy Church, and saw an invasion of privacy, which they struggled to believe they still kept.

3. Still she had come down the road toward the big white church alone. Just herself, an old forgetful woman, nearly blind with age. Just her and her eyes raised dully to the glittering cross that crowned the sheer silver steeple. She had walked along the road in a stagger from her house a half mile away. Perspiration, cold and clammy, stood on her brow and along the creases by her thin wasted nose. She stopped to calm herself on the wide front steps, not looking about her as they might have expected her to do, but simply standing quite still, except for a slight quivering of her throat and tremors that shook her cotton-stockinged legs.

4. The reverend of the church stopped her pleasantly as she stepped into the vestibule. Did he say, as they thought he did, kindly, "Auntie, you know this is not your church?" As if one could choose the wrong one. But no one remembers, for they never spoke of it afterward, and she brushed past him anyway, as if she had been brushing past him all her life, except this time she was in a hurry. Inside the church she sat on the very first bench from the back, gazing with concentration at the stained-glass window over her head. It was cold, even inside the church, and she was shivering. Everybody could see. They stared at her as they came in and sat down near the front. It was cold, very cold to them, too; outside the church it was below freezing and not much above inside. But the sight of her, sitting there somehow passionately ignoring them, brought them up short, burning.

5. The young usher, never having turned anyone out of his church before, but not even considering this job as *that* (after all, she had no right to be there, certainly), went up to her and whispered that she should leave. Did he call her "Grandma," as later he seemed to recall he had? But for those who actually hear such traditional pleasantries and to whom they actually mean something, "Grandma" was not one, for she did not pay him any attention, just muttered, "Go 'way," in a weak sharp *bothered* voice, waving his frozen blond hair and eyes from near her face.

6. It was the ladies who finally did what to them had to be done. Daring their burly indecisive husbands to throw the old colored woman out they made their point. God, mother, country, earth, church. It involved all that, and well they knew it. Leather bagged and shoed, with good calfskin gloves to keep out the cold, they looked with contempt at the bloodless gray arthritic hands of the old woman, clenched loosely, restlessly in her lap. Could their husbands expect them to sit up in church with *that*? No, no, the husbands were quick to answer and even quicker to do their duty.

7. Under the old woman's arms they placed their hard fists (which afterward smelled of decay and musk – the fermenting scent of onionskins and rotting greens). Under the old woman's arms they raised their fists, flexed their muscular shoulders, and out she flew through the door, back under the cold blue sky. This done, the wives folded their healthy arms across their trim middles and felt at once justified and scornful. But none of them said so, for none of them ever spoke of the incident again. Inside the church it was warmer. They sang, they prayed. The protection and promise of God's impartial love grew more not less desirable as the sermon gathered fury and lashed itself out above their penitent[3] heads.

[1] *giving way respectfully*   [2] *damaging*   [3] *repentant*

Imagine, explore, entertain: Writers from various cultures — Worksheet 17b

'The Welcome Table' (cont.) by Alice Walker (2)

8 The old woman stood at the top of the steps looking about in bewilderment. She had been singing in her head. They had interrupted her. Promptly she began to sing again, though this time a sad song. Suddenly, however, she looked down the long gray highway and saw something interesting and delightful coming. She started to grin, toothlessly, with short giggles of joy, jumping about and slapping her hands on her knees. And soon it became apparent why she was so happy. For coming down the highway at a firm though leisurely pace was Jesus. He was wearing an immaculate white, long dress trimmed in gold around the neck and hem, and a red, a bright red, cape. Over his left arm he carried a brilliant blue blanket. He was wearing sandals and a beard and he had long brown hair parted on the right side. His eyes, brown, had wrinkles around them as if he smiled or looked at the sun a lot. She would have known him, recognized him, anywhere. There was a sad but joyful look to his face, like a candle was glowing behind it, and he walked with sure even steps in her direction, as if he were walking on the sea. Except that he was not carrying in his arms a baby sheep, he looked exactly like the picture of him that she had hanging over her bed at home. She had taken it out of a white lady's Bible while she was working for her. She had looked at that picture for more years than she could remember, but never once had she really expected to see him. She squinted her eyes to be sure he wasn't carrying a little sheep in one arm, but he was not. Ecstatically she began to wave her arms for fear he would miss seeing her, for he walked looking straight ahead on the shoulder of the highway, and from time to time looking upward at the sky.

9 All he said when he got close to her was "Follow me," and she bounded down to his side with all the bob and speed of one so old. For every one of his long determined steps she made two quick ones. They walked along in deep silence for a long time. Finally she started telling him about how many years she had cooked for them, cleaned for them, nursed them. He looked at her kindly but in silence. She told him indignantly about how they had grabbed her when she was singing in her head and not looking, and how they had tossed her out of his church. A old heifer like me, she said, straightening up next to Jesus, breathing hard. But he smiled down at her and she felt better instantly and time just seemed to fly by. When they passed her house, forlorn and sagging, weatherbeaten and patched, by the side of the road, she did not even notice it, she was so happy to be out walking along the highway with Jesus.

10 She broke the silence once more to tell Jesus how glad she was that he had come, how she had often looked at his picture hanging on her wall (she hoped he didn't know she had stolen it) over her bed, and how she had never expected to see him down here in person. Jesus gave her one of his beautiful smiles and they walked on. She did not know where they were going; someplace wonderful, she suspected. The ground was like clouds under their feet, and she felt she could walk forever without becoming the least bit tired. She even began to sing out loud some of the old spirituals she loved, but she didn't want to annoy Jesus, who looked so thoughtful, so she quieted down. They walked on, looking straight over the treetops into the sky and the smiles that played over her dry wind-cracked face were like first clean ripples across a stagnant pond. On they walked without stopping.

11 The people in church never knew what happened to the old woman; they never mentioned her to one another or to anybody else. Most of them heard sometime later that an old colored woman fell dead along the highway. Silly as it seemed, it appeared she had walked herself to death. Many of the black families along the road said they had seen the old lady high-stepping down the highway; sometimes jabbering in a low insistent voice, sometimes singing, sometimes merely gesturing excitedly with her hands. Other times silent and smiling, looking at the sky. She had been alone, they said. Some of them wondered aloud where the old woman had been going so stoutly that it had worn her heart out. They guessed maybe she had relatives across the river, some miles away, but none of them really knew.

'Breaking into the Parthenon' (cont.) by Mark Twain (1)

SHORTLY we came upon an ancient stone aqueduct built upon arches, and from that time forth we had ruins all about us … We did not stop to inspect their massive blocks of marble or measure their height or guess at their extraordinary thickness, but passed at once through a great arched passage like a railway tunnel and went straight to the gate that leads to the ancient temples. It was locked! So, after all, it seemed that we were not to see the great Parthenon face to face. We sat down and held a council of war. Result: the gate was only a flimsy structure of wood – we would break it down. It seemed like desecration,[1] but then we had travelled far, and our necessities were urgent. We could not hunt up guides and keepers – we must be on the ship before daylight. So we argued. This was all very fine, but when we came to break the gate, we could not do it. We moved around an angle of the wall and found a low bastion:[2] eight feet high without, ten or twelve within. Denny prepared to scale it, and we got ready to follow. By dint of hard scrambling he finally straddled the top, but some loose stones crumbled away and fell with a crash into the court within. There was instantly a banging of doors and a shout. Denny dropped from the wall in a twinkling, and we retreated in disorder to the gate. **Xerxes** took that mighty citadel four hundred and eighty years before Christ, when his five millions of soldiers and camp followers followed him to Greece, and if we four Americans could have remained unmolested five minutes longer, we would have taken it too.

The garrison had turned out – four Greeks. We clamoured at the gate, and they admitted us. (Bribery and corruption.)

We crossed a large court, entered a great door, and stood upon a pavement of purest white marble, deeply worn by footprints. Before us in the flooding moonlight rose the noblest ruins we had ever looked upon – the **Propylaea**; a small Temple of **Minerva**; the Temple of **Hercules**; and the grand **Parthenon**. (We got these names from the Greek guide, who didn't seem to know more than seven men ought to know.) These edifices[3] were all built of the whitest **Pentelik** marble, but have a pinkish stain upon them now. Where any part is broken, however, the fracture looks like fine loaf sugar. Six **caryatids**, or marble women, clad in flowing robes, support the portico of the Temple of Hercules, but the **porticoes** and **colonnades** of the other structures are formed of massive **Doric** and **Ionic** pillars, whose **flutings** and **capitals** are still measurably perfect, notwithstanding the centuries that have gone over them and the sieges they have suffered. The Parthenon originally was two hundred and twenty-six feet long, one hundred wide, and seventy high, and had two rows of great columns, eight in each, at either end, and single rows of seventeen each down the sides, and was one of the most graceful and beautiful edifices ever erected …

[1] *damaging something sacred*   [2] *tower found at the angle of a fortification*   [3] *buildings*

Imagine, explore, entertain: Literary non-fiction

Worksheet 18b

'Breaking into the Parthenon' (cont.) by Mark Twain (2)

pg 28

Name
Form

The full moon was riding high in the cloudless heavens now. We sauntered carelessly and unthinkingly to the edge of the lofty battlements of the citadel and looked down – a vision! And such a vision! Athens by moonlight! The prophet that thought the splendours of the New Jerusalem[1] were revealed to him surely saw this instead! It lay in the level plain right under our feet – all spread abroad like a picture – and we looked down upon it as we might have looked from a balloon. We saw no semblance of a street, but every house, every window, every clinging vine, every projection, was as distinct and sharply marked as if the time were noonday; and yet there was no glare, no glitter, nothing harsh or repulsive – the noiseless city was flooded with the mellowest light that ever streamed from the moon, and seemed like some living creature wrapped in peaceful slumber. On its further side was a little temple, whose delicate pillars and ornate front glowed with a rich lustre that chained the eye like a spell; and nearer by, the palace of the king reared its creamy walls out of the midst of a great garden of shrubbery that was flecked all over with a random shower of amber lights – a spray of golden sparks that lost their brightness in the glory of the moon and glinted softly upon the sea of dark foliage like the pallid stars of the Milky Way. Overhead the stately columns, majestic still in their ruin – under foot the dreaming city – in the distance the silver sea – not on the broad earth is there another picture half so beautiful!

[1] *heavenly city*

Mark Twain is the pen name of Samuel Longhorne Clemens (1835–1910). His writing made him famous as the voice of frontier America. Before becoming a journalist, he worked as a steamboat pilot on the Mississippi, which is the source of his pen name: 'Mark Twain' is what the sailors shouted out when the water depth reached two fathoms. His most famous novel is *Huckleberry Finn*.

Imagine, explore, entertain: Literary non-fiction

Worksheet 19

Which dictionary to use? – analysis grid

pg 29

Name
Form

Using context to help you, complete this table by sorting the highlighted terms from the final section of the extract on **Worksheet 18a** into the four dictionary categories below. If you think a definition for a term might be found in more than one kind of dictionary, then place it in more than one column.

Standard school dictionary	Classical dictionary	Historical dictionary	Dictionary of architectural terms
	Parthenon		

Imagine, explore, entertain: Literary non-fiction

Worksheet 20

'Breaking into the Parthenon' – analysis grid

pg 29

Name:
Form:

Use this grid to analyse the poetic devices used by Mark Twain in the final paragraph of 'Breaking into the Parthenon'.

Poetic device	Examples from text	How it is effective
Alliteration		
Assonance		
Rhythm		
Repetition		
Onomatopoeia		
Imagery		
Simile		
Metaphor		
Personification		
Powerful words		

English Frameworking 3: Teacher's Resources © HarperCollins*Publishers* 2002

Imagine, explore, entertain: Literary non-fiction

Worksheet 21

Changing regular verbs into irregular ones

Name:
Form:

To help you prepare for writing a poem about irregular verbs, make these regular verbs irregular. Complete the grid with a regular verb that uses the same spelling pattern as an irregular verb in the present tense (e.g. 'bleed' and 'need'). Take the regular verb (e.g. 'need') and use the irregular verb's spelling pattern to form its past tense ('ned'). Run through the alphabet to locate your matching words:

A B C D E F G H I J K L M N O P Q R S T U V W X Y Z

Irregular verbs		Regular verbs that have same spelling pattern in present tense		
Present	Past	Present	Past	Past (made up)
bleed	bled	need	needed	(ned)
blow	blew			
catch	caught			
deal	dealt			
dig	dug			
eat	ate			
fall	fell			
freeze	froze			
get	got			
give	gave			
hear	heard	fear	feared	(feard – as in furd)
hold	held			
keep	kept			
make	made	bake	baked	(bade)
shake	shook	bake	baked	(book)
shine	shone			
shoot	shot			
sleep	slept			
speak	spoke			
steal	stole			
stick	stuck			
sting	stung			
strike	stroke			
sweep	swept			
teach	taught			
wake	woke			
win	won			
write	wrote			

| Imagine, explore, entertain: Literary non-fiction | Worksheet 22a |

'Bicycle Buying in Hungary' by Dervla Murphy (1)

Name:
Form:

First you find your bicycle, which is easy. Soon I saw what I wanted, hanging high in the window of a vast city-centre state store called Szivarvany. Model 153–421 was conspicuously marked 4,800 forints, then approximately $60. All the non-Soviet models cost at least 20,000 forints, an out-of-the-question investment since this machine was to be left with a Rumanian friend. Inside, hundreds of 153–421s were stacked along one wall in an alarmingly unassembled state: one would need an honours degree in engineering to get them on the road. In sign language I pleaded with a grumpy, undersized young man to sell me the assembled display model. He responded, naturally enough, in Hungarian, which language isolates its users to a unique extent from their fellow-Europeans. Yet his expression and tone conveyed a clear message: in this unreformed[1] state store no rule could possibly be bent for the sake of a mere customer. Despairingly I sought an English-speaker, or even a German- or French-speaker. In any Rumanian city multi-linguists would at once have swarmed, excitedly eager to help the foreigner. In Budapest it is otherwise.

Next I tried to coax the young man into himself assembling a bicycle for me. He looked scandalised[2] and dismissed the notion with a series of graphic gestures. Then he handed me a large twenty-four-page booklet in Russian, amply illustrated with twenty-six diagrams; the first showed a naked man standing beside my bicycle-to-be, measuring his legs against the wheels. Now came *my* graphic gestures, conveying horror and despair. The young man shrugged impatiently and produced a formidable document – five foolscap pages, hideously resembling an income tax return form. Presenting me with this sheaf, his manner suggested that now my problem was solved.

Page one was headed, in capitals: ELVESZETT JOTALLASI JEGYET CSAK AZ ELADAS NAPJANAK HITELT ERDEMLO IGAZOLASA (p1. DATUMMAL ES BELYEGZOVEL ELLATOTT SZAMLA, ELADASI JEGYZEK) ESETEN POTPLUNK! I wondered if the exclamation mark indicated that this was vital information needing at once to be absorbed by potential buyers of model 153–421.

Briskly the young man turned to another page, borrowed a pen and underlined VALLALAT BELYEGZOJE and ADOIGAZGATASI AZONOSITOSZAMA. I looked at him reproachfully, then took out my Angol–Magyar, Magyar–Angol *utiszotar*. It listed none of those words: the nearest was *azonos* ('identical') which shed no light on anything. At last the young man smiled; Hungarians appreciate, as well they might, even the feeblest of efforts to cope with their language. He then noticed a street plan in my shirt pocket. Spreading it on the counter, he indicated Egressy ut., wrote '17–21' in the margin, then turned to another page of the sheaf and there underlined *XIV Egressy ut., 17–21*. Semi-hysterically I giggled as the filler dropped. Of course! My purchase must be taken, with the sheaf, booklet and my receipt, to an establishment on the far side of Pest[3] where some genius would assemble it. Mine was not to reason why, mine but to do or die (almost) while wheeling model 153–421 through Budapest's traffic …

[1] *old-fashioned* [2] *shocked* [3] *The city of Budapest is in two halves, Buda and Pest, separated by the River Danube.*

| Imagine, explore, entertain: Literary non-fiction | Worksheet 22b |

'Bicycle Buying in Hungary' by Dervla Murphy (2)

No. 17–21 Egressy ut. was a strange left-over from the Communist era – at least I hope it was strange, not the sort of establishment Hungarians still have to combat on a daily basis. In a dreary barn-sized office men and women sat at metal desks, surrounded by tightly-packed filing cabinets. behind a bisecting counter … How, I wondered, was I going to negotiate those bureaucratic shoals <u>sans</u>¹ interpreter? But in fact the sheaf from Szivarvany, plus model 153–421, needed no verbal input from me. An elderly woman clerk, with glinting purple-copper hair such as one used to see on celluloid dolls, simply indicated where I was to sign another document guaranteeing that I could collect my property ten days hence.

I stared, appalled, at this rubber-stamped date – then smiled <u>ingratiatingly</u>² at the woman and boldly wrote in another, three days hence. The woman ground her teeth and struck out my date. Ten days or nothing, her expression said. And there was no charge; assembly was free and she wasn't interested in (or didn't understand?) my clumsy wordless hinting at a bribe. A dungaree-clad man then materialised at my elbow and wheeled model 153–421 away, beckoning me to follow. Scepticism took over when I saw my purchase joining hundreds – yes, *hundreds* – of unassembled clones. *Ten days*? More likely a month! I filled in the label presented by Dungarees, tied it to the handlebars as requested, was given yet another document – to be shown prior to collection – and went on my way, sorrowfully …

¹ *without*   ² *so as to gain favour*

Dervla Murphy was born in Co. Waterford, Ireland, of Dublin parents and still lives there. Since 1964 she has been regularly publishing descriptions of her journeys – by bicycle or on foot – in the remoter areas of four continents. She has also written about the problems of Northern Ireland, the hazards of the nuclear power industry and race relations in Britain.

Imagine, explore, entertain: Literary non-fiction — Worksheet 23

'Bicycle Buying in Hungary' – question sheet

pg 31

Name:
Form:

Question	Your answer	Evidence
1 What picture does the passage give you of life in Budapest?		
2 What does *Angol–Magyar Magyar–Angol utiszotar* mean?		
3 Underline the words and phrases that you think are effective in the second paragraph. What makes them so effective?		
4 What do you learn about the Hungarian language from this passage?		
5 How is this passage structured?		
6 What tone has the writer chosen to use?		
7 What do you learn about the writer from this passage?		
8 What do you think the writer's purpose was in writing this passage?		

English Frameworking 3: Teacher's Resources © HarperCollins Publishers 2002

69

A Tour Through the Whole of Great Britain by Daniel Defoe

Preface to the first volume

> If this work is not both pleasant and profitable to the reader, the author most freely and openly declares the fault must be in his performance, and it cannot be any deficiency in the subject. As the work it self is a description of the most flourishing and opulent[1] country in the world, so there is a flowing variety of materials; all the particulars are fruitful of instructing and diverting[2] objects.
>
> If novelty pleases, here is the present state of the country described, the improvement, as well in culture, as in commerce, the increase of people, and employment for them. Also here you have an account of the increase of buildings, as well as in great cities and towns, as in the new seats and dwellings of the nobility and gentry; also the increase of wealth in many eminent[3] particulars. If antiquity takes with you, though the looking back into remote things is studiously avoided, yet it is not wholly omitted, nor any useful observations neglected; the learned writers on the subject of antiquity in Great Britain have so well discharged themselves,[4] that we can never over-value their labours, yet there are daily farther discoveries made, which give future ages, room, perhaps not to mend, yet at least to add to what has already been done …

Letter 10 on Liverpool

> … Here is a ferry over the Mersee, which, at full sea, is more than two miles over. We land on the flat shore on the other side, and are contented to ride through the water for some length, not on horseback but on the shoulders of some honest Lancashire clown, who comes knee deep to the best side, to truss you up, and then runs away with you, as nimbly as you desire to ride, unless his trot were easier; for I was shaken by him that I had the luck to be carried by more than I cared for, and much worse than a hard trotting horse would have shaken me.
>
> Liverpoole is one of the wonders of Britain, and that more, in my opinion, than any of the wonders of the Peak; the town was at my first visiting it, about the year 1680, a large, handsome, well built and increasing or thriving town, at my second visit, anno[5] 1690, it was much bigger than at my first seeing it, and, by the report of the inhabitants, more than twice as big as it was twenty years before that; but, I think, I may safely say at this my third seeing of it, for I was surprised at the view, it was more than double what it was at the second; and, I am told, that it still visibly increases both in wealth, people, business and buildings. What it may grow to in time, I know not.
>
> There are no fortifications either to landward or seaward, the inhabitants resting secure under the protection of the general peace; though when the late northern insurrection[6] spread down their way, and came to Preston, they could have been glad of walls and gates; and indeed, had the rebel party had time to have advanced to Warrington, seized the pass there and taken Manchester, as they would certainly have done in three days more, it would have fared[7] but very ill with Liverpoole; who could have made but little resistance against an armed and desperate body of men, such as they appeared to be, and by that time would have been. But heaven had Liverpoole in its particular protection, as well as the whole kingdom; the rebels were met with, fought and defeated, before they gat leave to get so far, or to make any offer that way.
>
> The town has now an opulent, flourishing and increasing trade, not rivalling Bristol, in the trade to Virginia, and the English island colonies in America only, but is in a fair way to exceed and eclipse[8] it, by increasing every way in wealth and shipping. They trade round the whole island, send ships to Norway, to Hamburgh, and to the Baltick, as also to Holland and Flanders; so that, in a word, they are almost become like the Londoners, universal merchants.

[1] extremely wealthy [2] entertaining [3] distinguished, conspicuous [4] performed their task [5] in the year [6] uprising [7] gone [8] overshadow

> **Daniel Defoe** (1660–1731) is famous as a novelist and a pamphleteer. His most famous novels are *Robinson Crusoe* and *Moll Flanders*. His travel writing has made him an invaluable source of information about life in England at the end of the 17th century and the beginning of the 18th century.

Defoe and Bryson comparison cards

BILL BRYSON	DANIEL DEFOE
Purpose: To entertain	**Purpose:** To inform
Theme: Account of personal impressions and reflections while travelling around Britain.	**Theme:** Informative account of travels around Britain focusing on its appearance and economic developments, with related historical information where appropriate.
Style: *level of formality* Personal informal style using first person and some colloquial English.	**Style:** *level of formality* Impersonal formal style using third person as well as first person and formal English.
Style: *tone* Light-hearted; ironic	**Style:** *tone* Serious
Style: *sentence structure* Very short single clause sentences interspersed with more complex ones. Sentence pattern reflects spoken speech patterns.	**Style:** *sentence structure* Very long complex sentences interweaving subordinate clauses. One sentence over 75 words long. Uses semi-colon where full stop would be used today. Some unfamiliar phrasing.
Style: *vocabulary* Tends to use short familiar words.	**Style:** *vocabulary* Tends to use long unusual words.
Style: *spelling* Uses Standard English spelling.	**Style:** *spelling* Some words spelt differently from their modern English spelling.

Imagine, explore, entertain: Literary non-fiction

Worksheet 26

Notes from a Small Island by Bill Bryson

Chapter 19

I took a train to Liverpool. They were having a festival of litter when I arrived. Citizens had taken time off from their busy activities to add crisp packets, empty cigarette boxes, and carrier-bags to the otherwise bland and neglected landscape. They fluttered gaily in the bushes and brought colour and texture to pavements and gutters. And to think that elsewhere we stick these objects in rubbish bags …

Here's a piece of advice for you. Don't go on the Mersey ferry unless you are prepared to have the famous song by Gerry and the Pacemakers running through your head for about eleven days afterwards. They play it when you board the ferry and they play it when you get off and for quite a lot of time in between … Apart from that, it must be said that the Mersey ferry is an agreeable, if decidedly breezy, way of passing a morning. It's a bit like the Sydney Harbour cruise, but without Sydney.

When they weren't playing 'Ferry 'cross the Mersey', they played a soundtrack outlining the famous sights from the deck, but the acoustics were terrible and 80 per cent of whatever was said was instantly blown away on the wind. All I could hear were snatches of things like '3 million' and 'world's biggest' but whether they were talking about oil refinery capacity or Derek Hatton's suits[1] I couldn't say. But the gist of it was that *this* was once a great city and now it's Liverpool.

Now don't get me wrong. I'm exceedingly fond of Liverpool. It's probably my favourite English city. But it does rather feel like a place with more past than future. Leaning on a deck rail gazing out on miles of motionless waterfront, it was impossible to believe that until quite recently – and for two hundred proud and prosperous years before that – Liverpool's 10 miles of docks and shipyards provided employment for 100,000 people, directly or indirectly. Tobacco from Africa and Virginia, palm oil from the South Pacific, copper from Chile, jute from India, and almost any other commodity you could care to name passed through here on its way to being made into something useful. So too, no less significantly, did some ten million people bound for a new life in a new world, drawn by stories of streets paved with gold and the possibility of accumulating immense personal wealth, or in the case of my own forbears by the giddy prospect of spending the next century and a half dodging tornadoes and shovelling snow in Iowa …

The decline happened in a single generation. In 1966, Liverpool was still the second busiest port in Britain, after London. By 1985, it had fallen so low that it was smaller and quieter than even Tees and Hartlepool, Grimsby and Immingham. But in its heyday it was something special. Maritime commerce brought Liverpool not just wealth and employment, but an air of cosmopolitanism[2] that few cities in the world could rival, and it still has that sense about it. In Liverpool you still feel like you are some place.

I walked from the ferry to the Albert Dock. There were plans at one time to drain it and turn it into a car park – it seems a miracle sometimes that there is anything left in this poor, stumbling country – but now, of course, they have been scrubbed up and gentrified, the old warehouses turned into offices, flats and restaurants for the sort of people who carry telephones in their briefcases. It also incorporates an outpost of the Tate Gallery and the Mersey Maritime Museum.

Bill Bryson was born in Des Moines, Iowa, America in 1951. He became a journalist and settled in North Yorkshire in 1977 with his English wife and four children. At the end of the 1990s he moved back to America. He is the bestselling author of a range of travel writing, including *The Lost Continent*, *Notes from a Small Island* and *Walk in the Woods*. He has also written books on the development of the English language including *Mother Tongue*.

[1] *a Liverpool councillor famous for his lavish lifestyle*
[2] *representing all parts of the world*

Imagine, explore, entertain: Literary non-fiction — **Worksheet 27**

Spelling strategies

Name:
Form:

We all have different ways of learning. By now you should know which spelling strategies work best for you. Use the grid below to grade which spelling strategies are the most useful for you.

Strategy	Often use	Sometimes use	Never use	Words it has helped with
1 Break the word into sounds (e.g. e-n-t-e-r)				
2 Break the word into syllables (e.g. in-ter-est-ing)				
3 Break the word into its root and affixes (e.g. un-help-ful)				
4 Use a mnemonic (e.g 'In the end you need a friend')				
5 Apply spelling rules (e.g. 'i' before 'e' except after 'c' when the sound is 'ee' as in meet)				
6 Use spelling patterns (e.g. fright, slight, night, bright, etc.)				
7 Words in the same family (e.g. refer; referee, reference)				
8 Use analogy (e.g. where, there, here – all linked to 'place')				
9 Visual and aural memory (Look. Say. Cover. Write. Check)				
10 Use a base word (e.g. enjoyable/terrible for –able/–ible)				
11 Think about word origins – etymology (e.g. tri+angle = three angles)				
12 Mispronounce it to bring out the spelling (e.g. bus-i-ness; Parl-i-a-ment; sep-a-rate)				
13 Self checking – does it look right?				
14 Words within words (e.g. there's a 'rat' in separate)				
15 Pictures h+ ear = hear				

The categories of words that I can normally spell are:

The categories of words I often have problems with are:

Imagine, explore, entertain: Literary non-fiction — Worksheet 28

Sentence structure cards

Sentence starter introducing point	Linking phrase	Supporting evidence	Comment on significance
1 Bryson's witty tone and irony	can be illustrated by / is exemplified by	They were having a festival of litter when I arrived	This is effective because …. / This is entertaining because ….
2 Defoe's serious purpose	is summed up by / can be seen in	here is the present state of the country described	Such a statement makes it clear that …. / This immediately makes the reader think that ….

Imagine, explore, entertain: Literary non-fiction

Worksheet 29

Travel writing preparation

Name:

Form:

Vivid memory for descriptive passage

Entertaining incident or reflection

Location:

Information to be included

English Frameworking 3: Teacher's Resources © HarperCollinsPublishers 2002

Inform, explain, describe: Shakespeare play

Worksheet 30

Macbeth sequence cards

A During his royal banquet Macbeth learns that Banquo has been killed, but not Fleance. He is tormented by Banquo's ghost and Lady Macbeth has to send everyone home.

B Lady Macbeth encourages her husband to kill King Duncan while he is sleeping at their castle. Macbeth is anxious about doing the deed, but kills him anyway. Afterwards he is haunted by guilt.

C Macbeth becomes the new king of Scotland. Banquo is suspicious, but keeps quiet about what the witches had said in their prophecies.

D Macduff kills Macbeth, who dies bravely. Malcolm is proclaimed the next king of Scotland.

E On hearing that their father, King Duncan, has been murdered, Malcolm and Donalbain flee to England and Ireland for safety.

F On their journey home, after successfully defeating the invading Norwegian forces, noble soldiers Macbeth and Banquo are met on the heath by three witches, who tell them that Macbeth will become king and Banquo will be the father of future kings.

G Once he becomes king, Macbeth is worried that his friend Banquo knows his guilty secret and arranges to have him, and his son Fleance, killed.

H Scotland becomes torn apart by the evil King Macbeth, who kills all whom he suspects of being a threat. This includes the innocent wife and children of Macduff, who had gone to England to beg Malcolm to return and defeat Macbeth.

I Wanting to find out more about his future, Macbeth goes to see the witches. This time, although they give him a false sense of security, he becomes determined to destroy his enemies anyway.

J When they return to court, Macbeth and Banquo receive thanks and praise from King Duncan, but he formally announces that his son Malcolm is heir to the throne.

K While Macbeth is fighting Malcolm and Macduff's forces, Lady Macbeth, wracked with guilt for the evil she and her husband have done, commits suicide. Macbeth hears the news, but is beyond grief.

Inform, explain, describe: Shakespeare play

Worksheet 31

New words for old

pg 42

Name:
Form:

A

500 years ago verbs had yet to fall into a standard pattern. Look at those given below and write down the modern version of the past tense.

Past tense of Old English verb	Modern English verb	Past tense of modern verb
clomb	to climb	
knowed	to	
teared	to	
forgat	to	
digged	to	

1. What is the usual way in which the past tense is created?
2. Which of these verbs, past and present, are regular and which are irregular?

B

The spelling of some other words has remained the same, but they have come to mean something different. Look at the examples below and say what the modern meaning is.

Word	Old English meaning	Modern meaning
brave	cowardly	
garble	to sort something out	
manufacture	make something by hand	
awful	full of wonder	
artificial	skilfully done	

1. Discuss the link between the old and new meanings and try to explain the change.

C

Yet other words have fallen out of use altogether. Here are some that can be found in Shakespeare's plays but are no longer part of our everyday vocabulary. What might they have meant?

Shakespearean word	Meaning
batlet	
gallow	
pash	
mobled	
geck	

1. Why do you think these words fell out of use?
2. Are there any modern words that they may be connected with?

English Frameworking 3: Teacher's Resources © HarperCollins Publishers 2002

Inform, explain, describe: Shakespeare play

Worksheet 32

Fact and fiction in *Macbeth*

pg 43

Name:
Form:

True story of King Macbeth	Shakespeare's Macbeth	Why the facts were changed
1 Duncan was a young man probably in his late twenties when he died.	Duncan was an old man.	To make Macbeth appear more evil for killing Duncan, a harmless old man.
2 Duncan probably died of wounds he received in a battle against Macbeth.		
3 Macbeth and Lady Macbeth actually had a true claim to the Scottish throne which Duncan had usurped.		
4 Macbeth was king of Scotland for several years before Duncan's death.		
5 Macbeth was a strong and powerful king who ruled his country well for 17 years.		
6 Macbeth was a good man who went to Rome on pilgrimage and who gave money to the poor.		
7 Macbeth died from his wounds a while after the battle against Malcolm.		
8 Banquo was equally involved in bringing about the defeat and death of King Duncan.		
9 Lady Macbeth died some time after her husband.		
10 Lady Macbeth's death was from natural causes.		

English Frameworking 3: Teacher's Resources © HarperCollinsPublishers 2002

Inform, explain, describe: Shakespeare play

Worksheet 33a

Witches by e-mail (1)

pg 44

Name:
Form:

Write a series of e-mail messages that the witches might send to one another. To remain true to Shakespeare don't invent anything too far from the original script. The first one is done as an example.

From: weirdsis.one@spell.co.uk
To: weirdsis.two@spell.co.uk
cc: weirdsis.three@spell.co.uk
Subject: Win them to our charms

Message: Sisters dear, the three of us must meet soon to lure the gullible Macbeth and his friend. Great weather forecast – storms in Scotland all this week. Thunder and lightning – Thursday, or we could go for rain on Saturday. What is best? Please advise.

Act 1 scene 1

FIRST WITCH   When shall we three meet again?
              In thunder, lightning, or in rain?

From: weirdsis.two@spell.co.uk
To:
cc:
Subject:

Message:

SECOND WITCH   When the hurlyburly's done,
               When the battle's lost and won.

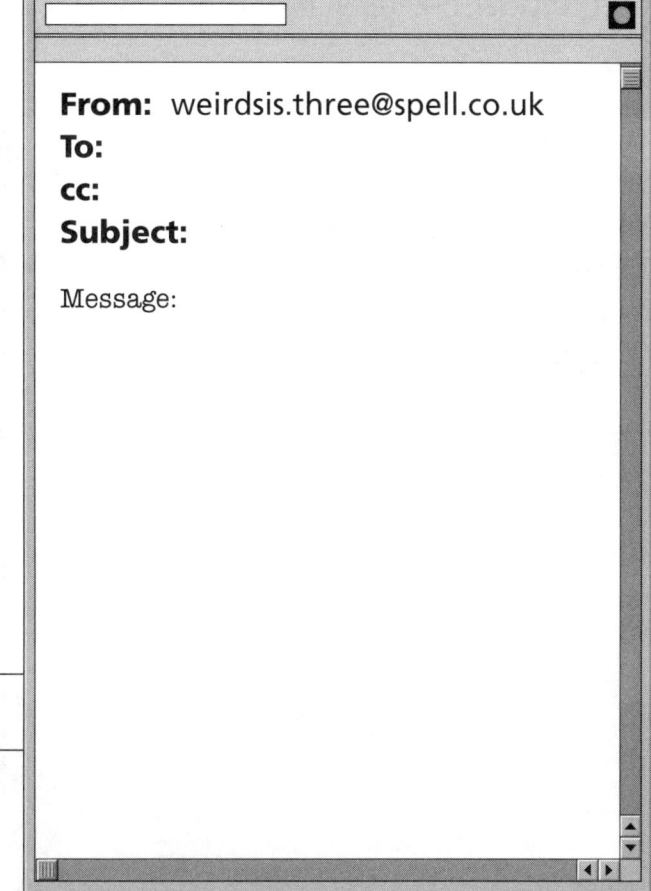

From: weirdsis.three@spell.co.uk
To:
cc:
Subject:

Message:

THIRD WITCH   That will be 'ere set of sun.

English Frameworking 3: Teacher's Resources   © HarperCollinsPublishers 2002

Inform, explain, describe: Shakespeare play

Worksheet **33b**

Witches by e-mail (2)

Name:
Form:

From: weirdsis.one@spell.co.uk
To:
cc:
Subject:

Message:

FIRST WITCH   Where the place?

From: weirdsis.two@spell.co.uk
To:
cc:
Subject:

Message:

SECOND WITCH   Upon the heath.

From: weirdsis.three@spell.co.uk
To:
cc:
Subject:

Message:

THIRD WITCH   There to meet with Macbeth.

Inform, explain, describe: Shakespeare play

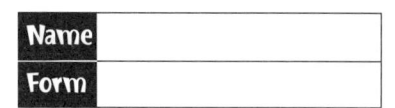

Worksheet 34

Macbeth's soliloquy (Act 2 scene 1)

MACBETH	Go bid thy mistress, when my drink is ready,	31
	She strike upon the bell. Get thee to bed.	

(Exit Servant)

Is this a dagger which I see before me,
The handle toward my hand? Come, let me clutch thee.
I have thee not, and yet I see thee still. 35
Art thou not, fatal vision, sensible
To feeling as to sight? or art thou but
A dagger of the mind, a false creation,
Proceeding from the heat-oppressed brain?
I see thee yet, in form as palpable 40
As this which now I draw.
Thou marshall'st me the way that I was going;
And such an instrument I was to use.
Mine eyes are made the fools o' th' other senses,
Or else worth all the rest. I see thee still; 45
And on thy blade and dudgeon gouts of blood,
Which was not so before. There's no such thing:
It is the bloody business which informs
Thus to mine eyes. Now o'er the one half-world
Nature seems dead, and wicked dreams abuse 50
The curtain'd sleep; witchcraft celebrates
Pale Hecate's offerings, and wither'd murder,
Alarum'd by his sentinel, the wolf,
Whose howl's his watch, thus with his stealthy pace,
With Tarquin's ravishing strides, towards his design 55
Moves like a ghost. Thou sure and firm-set earth,
Hear not my steps, which way they walk, for fear
Thy very stones prate of my whereabout,
And take the present horror from the time,
Which now suits with it. Whiles I threat, he lives; 60
Words to the heat of deeds too cold breath gives.

(A bell rings)

I go, and it is done; the bell invites me.
Hear it not, Duncan; for it is a knell
That summons thee to heaven or to hell.

(Exit)

Inform, explain, describe: Shakespeare play — Worksheet 35

Interpreting Shakespeare's words

Pair 1
MACBETH: angry, in a rage
LADY MACBETH: very fearful of Macbeth

Pair 2
MACBETH: tearful, as if he about to cry
LADY MACBETH: bossy, she is in charge

Pair 3
MACBETH: hard and in control, proud of what he has done
LADY MACBETH: evil, like a witch herself

Pair 4
MACBETH: bloodthirsty, revelling in his bloody hands
LADY MACBETH: anxious and worried

Pair 5
MACBETH: timid, afraid, very jumpy
LADY MACBETH: equally frightened

Pair 6
MACBETH: sounding evil and threatening
LADY MACBETH: cooing and gentle to keep him happy

Pair 7
MACBETH: slowly, like a lover come to boast
LADY MACBETH: drunk, not too sure what is going on

Pair 8
MACBETH: happy, elated
LADY MACBETH: proud of her husband

Pair 9
MACBETH: in a panic, stuttering
LADY MACBETH: very quickly as if they are about to be caught

Pair 10
MACBETH: quietly, like a conspirator
LADY MACBETH: high-spirited and cackling to herself

Inform, explain, describe: Shakespeare play

Worksheet 36

Macbeth Act 2 scene 2, lines 30–74

LADY MACBETH	Consider it not so deeply.	30
MACBETH	But wherefore could not I pronounce 'Amen'?	
	I had most need of blessing, and 'Amen'	
	Stuck in my throat.	
LADY MACBETH	These deeds must not be thought	
	After these ways; so, it will make us mad.	
MACBETH	Methought I heard a voice cry 'Sleep no more;	35
	Macbeth does murder sleep', — the innocent sleep,	
	Sleep that knits up the ravell'd sleave of care,	
	The death of each day's life, sore labour's bath,	
	Balm of hurt minds, great nature's second course,	
	Chief nourisher in life's feast.	
LADY MACBETH	What do you mean?	40
MACBETH	Still it cried 'Sleep no more' to all the house;	
	'Glamis hath murder'd sleep; and therefore Cawdor	
	Shall sleep no more — Macbeth shall sleep no more.'	
LADY MACBETH	Who was it that thus cried? Why, worthy Thane,	
	You do unbend your noble strength to think	45
	So brainsickly of things. Go get some water	
	And wash this filthy witness from your hand.	
	Why did you bring these daggers from the place?	
	They must lie there. Go carry them, and smear	
	The sleepy grooms with blood.	
MACBETH	I'll go no more:	50
	I am afraid to think what I have done;	
	Look on't again I dare not.	
LADY MACBETH	Infirm of purpose!	
	Give me the daggers. The sleeping and the dead	
	Are but as pictures; 'tis the eye of childhood	
	That fears a painted devil. If he do bleed,	55
	I'll gild the faces of the grooms withal;	
	For it must seem their guilt.	
	(Exit. Knocking within)	
MACBETH	Whence is that knocking?	
	How is't with me, when every noise appals me?	
	What hands are here? ha! they pluck out mine eyes.	
	Will all great Neptune's ocean wash this blood	60
	Clean from my hand? No; this my hand will rather	
	The multitudinous seas incarnadine,	
	Making the green one red.	
	(Re-enter LADY MACBETH)	
LADY MACBETH	My hands are of your colour; but I shame	
	To wear a heart so white. *(Knock)* I hear a knocking	65
	At the south entry; retire we to our chamber.	
	A little water clears us of this deed.	
	How easy is it then! Your constancy	
	Hath left you unattended. *(Knock)* Hark! more knocking.	
	Get on your nightgown, lest occasion call us	70
	And show us to be watchers. Be not lost	
	So poorly in your thoughts.	
MACBETH	To know my deed, 'twere best not know myself. *(Knock)*	
	Wake Duncan with thy knocking! I would thou couldst!	
	(Exeunt)	

Inform, explain, describe: Shakespeare play

Worksheet 37

Shakespeare's influence on language development

pg 48

Name
Form

Shakespeare had a phenomenal vocabulary and a talent for picking up new, interesting words and ones that had recently become fashionable. In fact 10 per cent of the words he used cannot be found before they appeared in his scripts. By incorporating them into his plays he ensured their popular use in his time and in the years to come. Without his influence many words would have fallen into disuse.

However, Shakespeare was not content with simply using his wide vocabulary: when there wasn't a word to suit his need, he coined a new one. To do this he drew on his classical education, a knowledge of Greek and Latin, to provide him with the roots for his new creations.

Here are some examples of the words and phrases that we have to thank Shakespeare for. They are now so much part of our everyday speech, it is difficult to imagine how we would do without them.

New words Shakespeare promoted	New words created by Shakespeare	Idioms and phrases we owe to Shakespeare
antipathy	barefaced	More in sorrow than in anger
critical	leapfrog	It's all Greek to me
demonstrate	monumental	Vanished into thin air
dire	obscene	Too much of a good thing
emphasis	dwindle	Early days
horrid	excellent	Bag and baggage
initiate	gust	The game is up
meditate	hint	Set your teeth on edge
modest	hurry	To give the devil his due
vast	lonely	Without rhyme or reason

If you want to find out more about how and why English has changed over time there are, among many good reference books, three very interesting sources:
- *Mother Tongue* by Bill Bryson, published by Penguin
- *The Story of English* by Robert McCrum, William Cran and Robert MacNeil, published by Faber and Faber
- *Fowler's Modern English Usage* edited by Sir Ernest Gowers, published by Oxford.

Inform, explain, describe: Shakespeare play

Worksheet **38a**

Macbeth Act 3 scene 4, lines 46–122 (1)

Name

Form

Macbeth has just learnt that his attempt to murder his friend Banquo and his son has only been partially successful, because Fleance has escaped. He learns this disturbing news during a banquet which he is giving for the noble lords of Scotland who have come to pay their respects to the newly crowned King Macbeth.

MACBETH	The table's full.	
LENNOX	Here is a place reserv'd, sir.	
MACBETH	Where?	
LENNOX	Here, my good lord.	
	What is't that moves your Highness?	
MACBETH	Which of you have done this?	
LORDS	What, my good lord?	
MACBETH	Thou canst not say I did it; never shake	50
	Thy gory locks at me.	
ROSS	Gentlemen, rise; his Highness is not well.	
LADY MACBETH	Sit, worthy friends. My lord is often thus,	
	And hath been from his youth. Pray you, keep seat.	
	The fit is momentary; upon a thought	55
	He will again be well. If much you note him,	
	You shall offend him and extend his passion.	
	Feed, and regard him not. — Are you a man?	
MACBETH	Ay, and a bold one that dare look on that	
	Which might appal the devil.	
LADY MACBETH	O proper stuff!	60
	This is the very painting of your fear;	
	This is the air-drawn dagger which you said	
	Led you to Duncan. O, these flaws and starts —	
	Impostors to true fear — would well become	
	A woman's story at a winter's fire,	65
	Authoriz'd by her grandam. Shame itself!	
	Why do you make such faces? When all's done,	
	You look but on a stool.	
MACBETH	Prithee, see there!	
	Behold! look! lo! how say you?	
	Why, what care I? If thou cans't nod, speak, too.	70
	If charnel-houses and our graves must send	
	Those that we bury back, our monuments	
	Shall be the maws of kites. *(Exit GHOST)*	
LADY MACBETH	What, quite unmann'd in folly?	
MACBETH	If I stand here, I saw him.	
LADY MACBETH	Fie, for shame!	
MACBETH	Blood hath been shed ere now, i' th' olden time,	75
	Ere humane statute purg'd the gentle weal;	
	Ay, and since too, murders have been perform'd	
	Too terrible for the ear. The time has been,	
	That when the brains were out the man would die,	
	And there an end; but now they rise again,	80
	With twenty mortal murders on their crowns,	
	And push us from our stools. This is more strange	
	Than such a murder is.	

Inform, explain, describe: Shakespeare play — Worksheet 38b

Macbeth Act 3 scene 4, lines 46–122 (2)

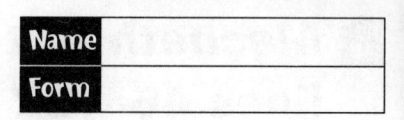

LADY MACBETH	My worthy lord, Your noble friends do lack you.
MACBETH	I do forget.

Do not muse at me, my most worthy friends; 85
I have a strange infirmity, which is nothing
To those that know me. Come, love and health to all;
Then I'll sit down. *(Enter GHOST)* Give me some wine, fill full.
I drink to the general joy o' th' whole table,
And to our dear friend Banquo, whom we miss. 90
Would he were here! To all, and him, we thirst,
And all to all.

LORDS　　　　　　　Our duties, and the pledge.
MACBETH　Avaunt, and quit my sight. Let the earth hide thee.
Thy bones are marrowless, thy blood is cold;
Thou hast no speculation in those eyes 95
Which thou dost glare with!

LADY MACBETH　　　　　　Think of this, good peers,
But as a thing of custom. 'Tis no other;
Only it spoils the pleasure of the time.

MACBETH　What man dare, I dare.
Approach thou like the rugged Russian bear, 100
The arm'd rhinoceros, or th' Hyrcan tiger;
Take any shape but that, and my firm nerves
Shall never tremble. Or be alive again,
And dare me to the desert with thy sword;
If trembling I inhabit, then protest me 105
The baby of a girl. Hence, horrible shadow!
Unreal mock'ry, hence!
(Exit GHOST)
　　　　　　　Why, so; being gone,
I am a man again. Pray you, sit still.

LADY MACBETH　You have displac'd the mirth, broke the good meeting,
With most admir'd disorder.

MACBETH　　　　　　　Can such things be, 110
And overcome us like a summer's cloud,
Without our special wonder? You make me strange
Even to the disposition that I owe,
When now I think you can behold such sights
And keep the natural ruby of your cheeks, 115
When mine is blanch'd with fear.

ROSS　　　　　　　What sights, my lord?
LADY MACBETH　I pray you, speak not; he grows worse and worse;
Question enrages him. At once, good night.
Stand not upon the order of your going,
But go at once.

LENNOX　　　　　　Good night; and better health 120
Attend his majesty!

LADY MACBETH　　　　　　A kind good night to all!
(Exeunt LORDS and ATTENDANTS)

> Inform, explain, describe: Shakespeare play

Worksheet 39

Gathering the evidence for your essay

pg 50

Name:
Form:

Use the following as guidelines to help you explore the scenes in an organized way. Make notes about things which strike you as being particularly interesting, and include direct quotations where they are appropriate.

Purpose and plot

Why did Shakespeare include these particular scenes in his play?

Themes and topics

What themes and topics does Shakespeare introduce that you find interesting?
(E.g. guilt, ambition, good and evil, order and disorder in society.)

> Explain how Shakespeare interests and entertains audiences in the three key scenes you have studied in *Macbeth*:
> - Act 2 scenes 1 and 2,
> - Act 3 scene 4.

Characters

(E.g. How do the characters and the interaction between them hold your interest during the play?)

Language and imagery

How does Shakespeare use the power of language to interest the audience?
(E.g. the use of description and imagery, or powerful dialogue between characters.)

Dramatic technique

What dramatic devices does Shakespeare use to attract your attention?
(E.g. the use of the supernatural, dramatic irony, soliloquy.)

English Frameworking 3: Teacher's Resources © HarperCollins Publishers 2002

Inform, explain, describe: Shakespeare play

Worksheet 40

Planning your essay

Name
Form

> Explain how Shakespeare interests and entertains audiences with reference to the three key scenes you have studied in *Macbeth*:
> - Act 1 scenes 1 and 2,
> - Act 3 scene 4.

Introduction Begin by showing that you have understood the question.

In 'Macbeth' Shakespeare engages the interest of the audience by …

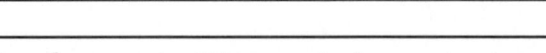

Development What made the greatest impression on you?
Write in more detail about the things you think are the strongest points.

The audience would be most impressed by the …

What other factors add interest? Give less detail on the points that you think are not as strong as the ones mentioned above.

In addition the …

Alternative What do you think was a weakness as far as you were concerned?

However, …

Conclusion Weigh up the points you made earlier and offer an overall comment and summary of what you think the strongest points are in response to the task you were originally set.

Although Macbeth was written 400 years ago, Shakespeare's play can still interest 21st-century audiences …

88

English Frameworking 3: Teacher's Resources   © HarperCollins Publishers 2002

Inform, explain, describe: Media texts

Worksheet 41

Evaluating the EPA website home page on global warming

pg 52

Name
Form

1 How does the page strike you at first glance, for example is it attractive, well laid out, cluttered or dull?	
2 Does the site look straightforward to use, for example is it easy to read, hard to follow, unclear?	
3 Is it obvious whose website this is?	
4 Can you easily identify the topic that it is covering?	
5 If you wanted to find particular information about certain aspects of the topic such as climate change or the greenhouse effect would you know where to look?	
6 If you came from a group with a particular interest, such as someone who lived on the coast or someone who was interested in wildlife protection, where would you be able to find information tailored to meet your needs?	
7 Is it obvious that certain areas of the page are active and would link you to other pages? If you were online, how could you tell?	
8 Do you think you would be able to navigate around the site easily to find the information you needed and be able to find your way back to the home page? Would you be able to move from one page to another with ease? What would help you to do this?	
9 What improvements would you make to this home page? Is there any way you could inform the EPA of any suggestions you might have?	
10 What is your overall assessment of this home page?	

English Frameworking 3: Teacher's Resources © HarperCollinsPublishers 2002

Inform, explain, describe: Media texts

Worksheet 42

World at Risk! Website Challenge

pg 53

Name
Form

A group of concerned individuals from the international business world have issued a challenge to teenagers, to create a website designed to make young people between the ages of 11–14 around the world become more active and concerned about the following global issues:

1 **Rainforest at risk!** How can we stop the destruction of Amazonian rainforest?
2 **Whales at risk!** How can we prevent the revival of the whaling industry?
3 **Children at risk!** How can we help children around the world whose rights are being ignored?

Your group will be designing a website for one of these issues which will:
- Inform people about the topic you have chosen
- Explain the issues that are involved
- Describe what people can do to help.

Members of our group:

Issues linked with our chosen topic that we need to investigate are:

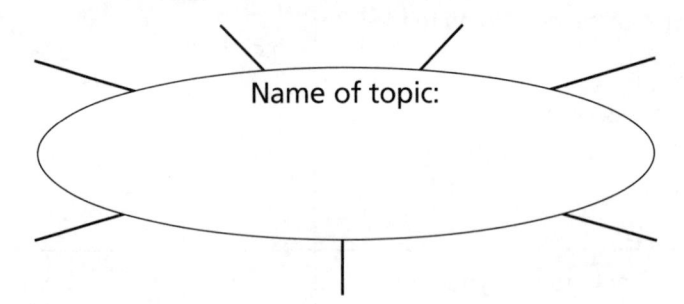

Name of topic:

Questions we need to answer are:
-
-
-
-

My responsibility will be to:

Inform, explain, describe: Media texts

Worksheet 43

Paul Brown on global warming

Name:
Form:

Melt down

Five years ago in a book about global warming, I posed the question "Can Civilisation Survive?" I genuinely did not know the answer. 1996 was the year before the world agreed to legally binding greenhouse emissions' targets in Kyoto and when the speed and extent of climate change was still very uncertain.

As politicians from around the world meet in Bonn to try to rescue the climate talks from failure, Paul Brown reviews the snail-pace of progress and considers the future

Climate science was developing backwards and forwards. New discoveries allowed calculations about what the atmosphere used to be like – examined with the aid of ancient tree rings and ice cores taken from Greenland and the Antarctic. This information and current observations of steadily rising temperatures and greenhouse gas levels were fed into computers to provide ever more sophisticated models of what was going to happen in the future.

Scientists have made remarkable progress in both predictions and the certainty of their calculations. They have not just looked at the temperatures and sea level rise but such issues as rainfall, wind storms and droughts. The effects on water availability, ability to grow crops, even such things as glacier melt providing summer water supply have been minutely examined and calculated. Tree growth, due to increased carbon dioxide, has been measured against losses caused by excess heat, or forest moving north as the tundra melts. On the whole, the picture is one of increasing and more uncontrollable disasters, almost unmitigated bad news for the poorest and already disadvantaged developing world, and hardly much better for anyone else.

Once scientists used to refer to the effects of global warming being bad for our grandchildren. Five years ago they began to talk about our children, and now we are already seeing the effects. Last winter's floods in the UK were openly ascribed to a change in the weather caused by global warming. It could just have been a fluke, coinciding with the predictions, but one flood in a 100 years can now be expected every five or 10 years, or possibly more often.

Scientists are saying that this is only the beginning. It will get far worse quite quickly. To be on the safe side we should cut greenhouse gas emissions by 60 to 80% by the middle of the century to stabilise the climate before things get out of hand. It will get much warmer and the sea level will continue to rise for another 300 years or so because of the melting of the ice caps.

The public, and some journalists who failed to research the subject, rather liked the idea of not having to go to Tuscany for their holidays and drinking wines produced from vines in their own back gardens. But the brutal reality of some of the filthy weather that has become commonplace across Europe has changed the public's mind. The threat of global warming has become real.

Even in the US, which in this sense is a backward country, the connection between the fires of last summer, other extreme weather events and global warming has become a topic of conversation. In the last five years companies like Ford, oil companies like BP and Shell have begun to pour billions into research in new technologies. Wind power is now mainstream, solar is in rapid development, hybrid cars are on the road. Cars that run on fuel cells, hydrogen and compressed air are no longer pipe dreams, they are close to mass production.

Industry was looking to the Kyoto process and the next steps that go beyond it – targets of 20% reduction of carbon dioxide by 2020 and more after that – to push the new technologies forward. Some believe with the collapse of the talks of the last six months the momentum has been lost, but most believe the investment is already too great to be lost now. So despite the apparent lack of progress in international agreement and abject failure of political will, there is an advance and there are champions in unlikely places.

But this is not enough. If the scientists are right, then the human race is not running fast enough to escape the calamity it has created. When I asked that question about whether civilisation could survive, I did not know. Now I'm certain that on the evidence, and the appalling lack of political leadership, the answer has to be no. Drought, disaster, famine, failure of banks will plunge the world into economic turmoil before we have time to turn the climate juggernaught around. It won't be the end of the world, but it will be a very different place than it is now.

from The Guardian July 18, 2001

Guardian Unlimited © Guardian Newspapers Limited 2001

Paul Brown is the Guardian's environment correspondent

Inform, explain, describe: Media texts

Worksheet 44

EPA global warming site map

pg 56

Name
Form

One of the buttons on the right-hand side of the home page of the EPA site is called 'Kids and Educators'. If a user clicks on the Kids section of this button, the hyperlink will take them immediately to the pages linked with this aspect of the site. As this is a big website there is a Kids home page, like a sub-directory, with new buttons to click, indicating new areas that can be explored and new pages that can be called to the screen. Buttons at the bottom of every page of the website enable the visitor to return to the home page; the back navigation button at the top of the computer screen can also be used to retrace your steps.

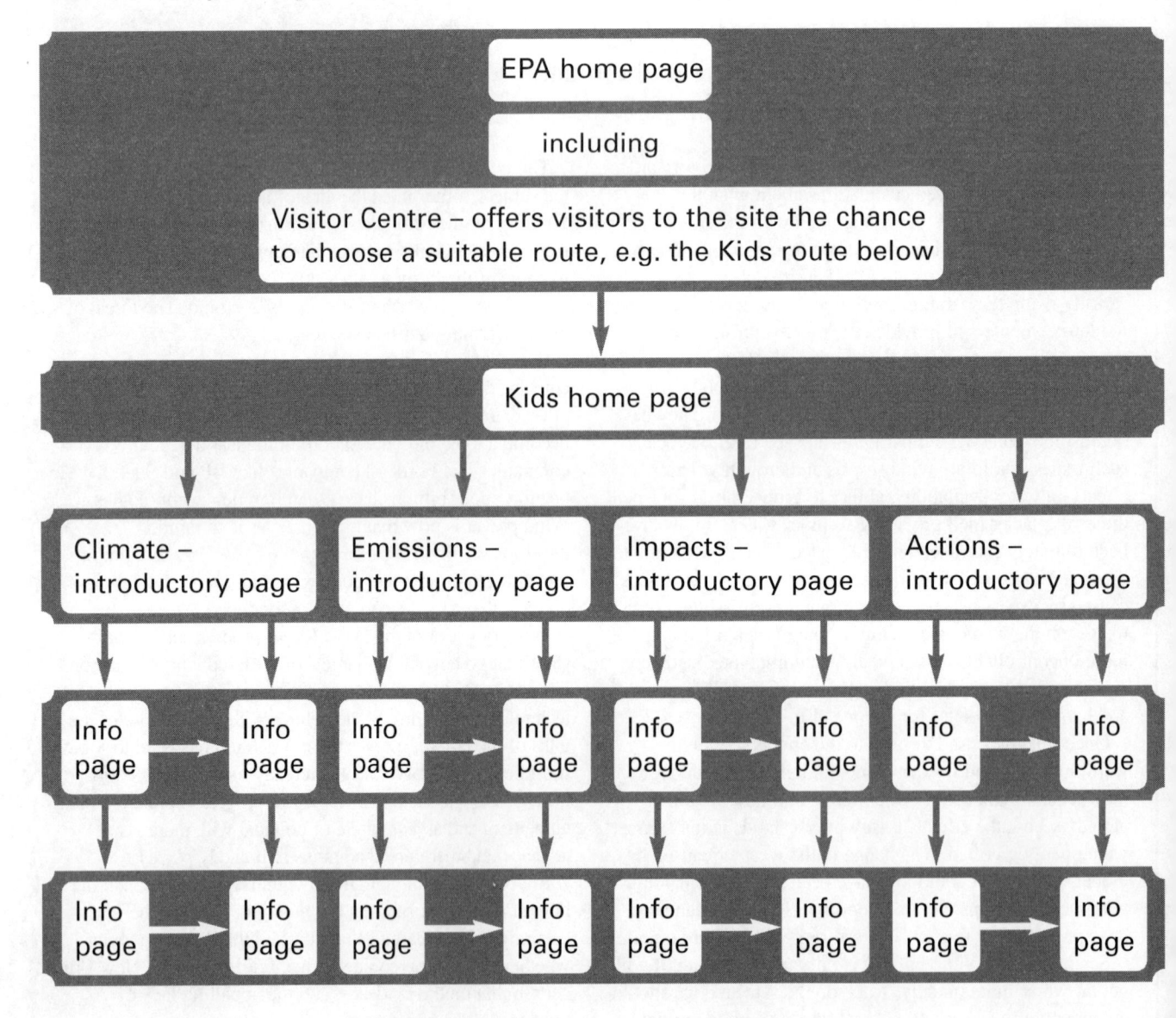

```
                    EPA home page
                        including
   Visitor Centre – offers visitors to the site the chance
   to choose a suitable route, e.g. the Kids route below
                            ↓
                     Kids home page
         ↓              ↓              ↓              ↓
    Climate –      Emissions –      Impacts –      Actions –
 introductory   introductory    introductory    introductory
     page           page            page            page
      ↓   ↓        ↓   ↓          ↓   ↓          ↓   ↓
   Info→Info    Info→Info      Info→Info      Info→Info
   page page    page page      page page      page page
    ↓    ↓       ↓    ↓         ↓    ↓         ↓    ↓
   Info→Info→Info→Info→Info→Info→Info→Info
   page page page page page page page page
```

92

English Frameworking 3: Teacher's Resources © HarperCollinsPublishers 2002

Inform, explain, describe: Media texts

Worksheet 45

EPA kids site – the greenhouse effect

Name
Form

EPA United States Environmental Protection Agency

Games!
Links!

GLOBAL WARMING

Kids Site

Greenhouse Effect...

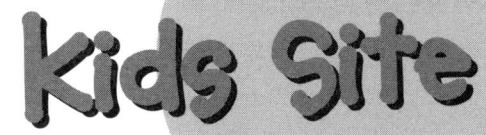

- Global Warming (What it is)
- Climate & Weather
- Greenhouse Effect
- What is the Climate System?
- Climate's come a LONG WAY!
- The Climate Detectives ...
- Can we Change the Climate?
- So What's the BIG DEAL?
- We CAN Make a Difference!

The greenhouse effect is the rise in the temperature that the Earth experiences because certain gases in the atmosphere (water vapor, carbon dioxide, nitrous oxide, and methane, for example) trap energy from the sun. Without these gases, heat would escape back into space and Earth's temperature would be about 60°F colder. Because of how they warm our world, these gases are referred to as greenhouse gases.

Have you ever seen a greenhouse? Most greenhouses look like a small glass house. Greenhouses are used to grow plants, especially in the winter. Greenhouses work by trapping heat from the sun. The glass panels of the greenhouse let in light but keep heat from escaping. This causes the greenhouse to heat up, much like the inside of a car parked in the sunlight, and keeps the plants warm enough to live in the winter.

The Earth's atmosphere is all around us. It is the air that we breath. Greenhouse gases in the the atmosphere behave much like the glass panes in a greenhouse. Sunlight enters the Earth's atmosphere, passing through the blanket of greenhouse gases. As it reaches the Earth's surface, land, water and biosphere absorb the sunlight's energy. Once absorbed, the energy is sent back into the atmosphere. Some of the energy passes back into space, but much of it remains trapped in the atmosphere by the greenhouse gases, causing our world to heat up.

The greenhouse effect is important. Without the greenhouse effect, the Earth would not be warm enough for humans to live. But if the greenhouse effect becomes stronger, it could make the Earth warmer than usual. Even a little extra warming may cause problems for humans, plants, and animals.

next ...

The Greenhouse Effect

Solar radiation passes through the clear atmosphere.

Most radiation is absorbed by the earth's surface and warms it.

Some solar radiation is reflected by the earth and the atmosphere.

Some of the infrared radiation passes through the atmosphere, and some is absorbed and re-emitted in all directions by greenhouse gas molecules. The effect of this is to warm the earth's surface and the lower atmosphere.

Infrared radiation is emitted from the earth's surface.

Home || Glossary || Comments || Search || US EPA
http:/www.epa.gov/globalwarming/kids/greenhouse.html
Last Updated on April 6, 2001

Inform, explain, describe: Media texts

Worksheet 46

Website evaluation form

Name: _____
Form: _____

Website address (URL): _____

Website name: _____

Today's date: _____

Accessibility
Is it easy to navigate through this site and did the links work? _____
_____

Accuracy
1 Source
   - Where does the information come from? _____
   - How might you check to make sure it's real? _____

2 Authority
   - Who created the site (the name is usually at the top or very bottom)? _____
   _____
   - Does the author belong to an organization which adds credibility to the site?
     Which organization is it? _____
   _____

3 Objectivity
   - Does the information seem biased? _____
   - Why or why not? _____

4 Coverage
   - Is there enough information about the topic, or do you need more? _____
   - Is there more information than you would find in an encyclopaedia? _____

Appropriateness
Is the information written for students or experts? Can you understand the information?
_____

Appeal
Is the site colourful, easy to read, full of graphics, and fun to use? _____
_____

Conclusion
Are you confident using this source for your research? Would you use this site again and recommend it to a friend to use for a school project?
_____
_____
_____

Inform, explain, describe: Media texts | Worksheet 47

High North Alliance home page

Name:
Form:

HIGH NORTH WEB

HIGH NORTH ALLIANCE

ARGUMENTS, FACTS and NEWS

Working for the future of coastal cultures and the sustainable use of marine resources

::: More about us :::

MAINMENU

HOME

LIBRARY

ARGUMENTATION

THE SHOP

HARPOON CARTOONS

GUESTBOOK

CONTACT US

PUBLICATIONS

LINKS

Support the High North Alliance as a member

HEADLINES

29.08.2001:
Norwegian whaling season draws to a successful close
2001 will end up as a year Norwegian whalers remember well, as the full quota will probably be taken for the first time in years.
more...

29.08.2001:
Hunters-art too controversial for the UK
"Hunters of the North" is the modest title of an exhibition galleries and museums in Scotland are afraid of allowing onto their premises. 'The word "hunter" is obviously taboo in the UK,' says Birgir Kruse, the co-ordinator of the exhibition.
more...

24.8.2001:
More Pilot Whale Meat and Blubber for City People
The capital city of Tórshavn in the Faroes is now using a new system to distribute pilot whale meat and blubber to its residents.
more...

15.08.2001:
"Cockroach" man's new book, out now!
Masayuki Komatsu, a senior Japanese fisheries official, who recently hit the international media for comparing the fertility of minke whale stocks of the Southern Ocean with the fertility of cockroaches, has just released a new book: The Truth Behind the Whaling Dispute.
more...

FOCUS

Photo gallery

::: NEWS ARCHIVE :::

`Search news database` [GO]

::: HIGH NORTH ALLIANCE, P.O. Box 123, N-8398 Reine i Lofoten, Norway :::

Inform, explain, describe: Media texts

Worksheet 48

CRIN home page

Name
Form

search | about CRIN | join CRIN | for members | contact us

CRIN
child rights information network

child rights
- Convention of the Rights of the Child
- NGO Alternative Reports
- International Treaties

resources
- E-mail Lists
- Events
- News
- Publications

organisations
- All Organisations
- CRIN Members
- NGO Group for CRC

regional information
- Africa
- Asia
- Central America & Caribbean
- Europe
- Middle East
- North America
- Oceania
- South America

New! CRIN Newsletter 14: Special Session on Children

The Convention on the Rights of the Child treaty spells out the basic human rights that children everywhere – without discrimination – have:

- the right to survival;
- to develop to the fullest;
- to protection from harmful influences, abuse and exploitation;
- to participate fully in family, cultural and social life.

The key objectives of the Child Rights Information Network are to improve the lives of children by:

- meeting the information needs of organisations and individuals working for child rights
- supporting and promoting the implementation of the Convention on the Rights of the Child
- developing networking tools that enable effective information exchange among members of CRIN

The CRIN programme for child rights includes:

- Website: Containing references to hundreds of publications, recent news and upcoming events, as well as details of organisations working worldwide for children. The site also includes NGO reports submitted to the UN Committee on the Rights of the Child.
- Email list service: Distributed twice a week in English, French and Spanish, CRINMAIL provides regular news bulletins about child rights issues, new publications and upcoming events.
- Regional Information: CRIN is working with partners in Africa, the Americas, Asia, the Arab World and Europe in order to promote child rights worldwide.
- Newsletter: Published three times a year, the CRIN Newsletter is a thematic publication that examines a specific issue affecting children. Available in English, French and Spanish it summarises relevant news, events, publications and campaigns.

Search the CRIN website:

[ ] search

themes
- About child rights
- Armed conflict
- Child labour
- Disability
- Discrimination
- Education
- Health
- HIV/AIDS
- Juvenile Justice
- Macroeconomics
- Media
- Sexual exploitation
- UN Special Session on Children
- Violence against children

Inform, explain, describe: Media texts — **Worksheet 49**

Website Challenge evaluation sheet

pg 61

Name:
Form:

Name of website being evaluated:

Members of the evaluating group:

Criteria	Score/5	Comments
1 The **home page** makes the purpose, target audience and the cause that the website is supporting clear.		
2 The website is **accessible** – it is easy to see how a visitor would find further information and be able to navigate to these points.		
3 The website has made good use of **presentational and stylistic** features such as bullet points, fonts, italics, etc.		
4 The material is **appropriate** – the needs of the target audience have been specifically addressed.		
5 The information is **accurate** – it appears to have been properly researched and acknowledges sources and authors.		
6 The **link pages** have properly addressed their specific focus, the information is adequate and interesting.		
7 The website as a whole is **appealing** – good colour, pictures, graphics, etc.		
Overall score:		
General comments:		

English Frameworking 3: Teacher's Resources   © HarperCollins Publishers 2002

Persuade, argue, advise: English literary heritage

Famous writers and their works

Jane Austen	*Daffodils*
Charlotte Brontë	*Robinson Crusoe*
Geoffrey Chaucer	*Romeo and Juliet*
Daniel Defoe	*Frankenstein*
Charles Dickens	*Paradise Lost*
John Milton	*Jane Eyre*
George Orwell	*Treasure Island*
William Shakespeare	*The Importance of Being Earnest*
Mary Shelley	*Oliver Twist*
Robert Louis Stevenson	*Pride and Prejudice*
Oscar Wilde	*Canterbury Tales*
William Wordsworth	*Animal Farm*

Worksheet 50

English Frameworking 3: Teacher's Resources © HarperCollins Publishers 2002

Persuade, argue, advise: English literary heritage

Worksheet 51a

Pride and Prejudice by Jane Austen (1)

Chapter 1

It is a truth universally acknowledged, that a single man in possession of a good fortune, must be in want of a wife.

However little known the feelings or views of such a man may be on his first entering a neighbourhood, this truth is so well fixed in the minds of the surrounding families, that he is considered as the rightful property of some one or other of their daughters.

'My dear Mr Bennet,' said his lady to him one day, 'have you heard that Netherfield Park is let at last?'

Mr Bennet replied that he had not.

'But it is,' returned she; 'for Mrs Long has just been here, and she told me all about it.'

Mr Bennet made no answer.

'Do not you want to know who has taken it?' cried his wife impatiently.

'*You* want to tell me, and I have no objection to hearing it.'

This was invitation enough.

'Why, my dear, you must know, Mrs Long says that Netherfield is taken by a young man of large fortune from the north of England; that he came down on Monday in a chaise and four[1] to see the place, and was so much delighted with it that he agreed with Mr Morris immediately; that he is to take possession before Michaelmas, and some of his servants are to be in the house by the end of next week.'

'What is his name?'

'Bingley.'

'Is he married or single?'

'Oh! single, my dear, to be sure! A single man of large fortune; four or five thousand a year. What a fine thing for our girls!'

'How so? how can it affect them?'

'My dear Mr Bennet,' replied his wife, 'how can you be so tiresome! You must know that I am thinking of his marrying one of them.'

'Is that his design in settling here?'

'Design! nonsense, how can you talk so! But it is very likely that he *may* fall in love with one of them, and therefore you must visit him as soon as he comes.'

'I see no occasion for that. You and the girls may go, or you may send them by themselves, which perhaps will be still better, for as you are as handsome as any of them, Mr Bingley might like you the best of the party.'

'My dear, you flatter me. I certainly *have* had my share of beauty, but I do not

[1] *horse-drawn carriage*

Pride and Prejudice by Jane Austen (2)

pretend to be any thing extraordinary now. When a woman has five grown up daughters, she ought to give over thinking of her own beauty.'

'In such cases, a woman has not often much beauty to think of.'

'But, my dear, you must indeed go and see Mr Bingley when he comes into the neighbourhood.'

'It is more than I engage for,[1] I assure you.'

'But consider your daughters. Only think what an establishment it would be for one of them. Sir William and Lady Lucas are determined to go, merely on that account, for in general you know they visit no new comers. Indeed you must go, for it will be impossible for *us* to visit him, if you do not.'

'You are over scrupulous,[2] surely. I dare say Mr Bingley will be very glad to see you; and I will send a few lines by you to assure him of my hearty consent to his marrying which ever he chuses of the girls; though I must throw in a good word for my little Lizzy.'

'I desire you will do no such thing. Lizzy is not a bit better than the others; and I am sure she is not half so handsome as Jane, nor half so good humoured as Lydia. But you are always giving *her* the preference.'

'They have none of them much to recommend them,' replied he; 'they are all silly and ignorant like other girls; but Lizzy has something more of quickness than her sisters.'

'Mr Bennet, how can you abuse your own children in such a way? You take delight in vexing me. You have no compassion on my poor nerves.'

'You mistake me, my dear. I have a high respect for your nerves. They are my old friends. I have heard you mention them with consideration these twenty years at least.'

'Ah! you do not know what I suffer.'

'But I hope you will get over it, and live to see many young men of four thousand a year come into the neighbourhood.'

'It will be no use to us, if twenty such should come since you will not visit them.'

'Depend upon it, my dear, that when there are twenty, I will visit them all.'

Mr Bennet was so odd a mixture of quick parts, sarcastic humour, reserve, and caprice,[3] that the experience of three and twenty years had been insufficient to make his wife understand his character. *Her* mind was less difficult to develop. She was a woman of mean[4] understanding, little information and uncertain temper. When she was discontented she fancied herself nervous. The business of her life was to get her daughters married; its solace[5] was visiting and news.

[1] *promise to do* [2] *careful and correct in behaviour* [3] *whim, changeable behaviour* [4] *small* [5] *comfort*

Persuade, argue, advise: English literary heritage — Worksheet 52

Pride and Prejudice – analysis grid

Name:
Form:

Use this grid to analyse the opening chapter of Jane Austen's *Pride and Prejudice*.

Aspect being considered	Point	Evidence	Comment
1 What is the tone of the first two paragraphs? Is the author being serious or wanting to entertain her readers?			
2 How can you tell that this is not a genteel, 21st-century couple speaking?			
3 What do you learn about Mrs Bennet's character from this chapter?			
4 What do you learn about Mr Bennet's character from this chapter?			
5 What clues are there for how the plot will develop?			

English Frameworking 3: Teacher's Resources   © HarperCollins*Publishers* 2002

101

Persuade, argue, advise: English literary heritage

Worksheet 53

KWL grid: Charles Dickens

Name
Form

What do I know about Charles Dickens?	What do I want to know about the opening chapter of Great Expectations?			
		How has Dickens structured the opening of *Great Expectations*?	What ingredients has Dickens included in the opening of *Great Expectations*?	How does Dickens build up the reader's sympathy with the convict even though he has threatened young Pip?
	What have I learnt?			

English Frameworking 3: Teacher's Resources   © HarperCollins*Publishers* 2002

| Persuade, argue, advise: English literary heritage | Worksheet 54a |

Great Expectations by Charles Dickens (1)

Ours was the marsh country, down by the river, within, as the river wound, twenty miles of the sea. My first most vivid and broad impression of the identity of things, seems to me to have been gained on a memorable raw afternoon towards evening. At such a time I found out for certain, that this bleak place overgrown with nettles was the churchyard; and that Philip Pirrip, late of this parish, and also Georgiana wife of the above, were dead and buried; and that Alexander, Bartholomew, Abraham, Tobias, and Roger, infant children of the aforesaid, were also dead and buried; and that the dark flat wilderness beyond the churchyard, intersected with dykes and mounds and gates, with scattered cattle feeding on it, was the marshes; and that the low leaden line beyond was the river; and that the distant savage lair from which the wind was rushing, was the sea; and that the small bundle of shivers growing afraid of it all and beginning to cry, was Pip.

'Hold your noise!' cried a terrible voice, as a man started up from among the graves at the side of the church porch. 'Keep still, you little devil, or I'll cut your throat!'

A fearful man, all in coarse grey, with a great iron on his leg. A man with no hat, and with broken shoes, and with an old rag tied round his head. A man who had been soaked in water, and smothered in mud, and lamed by stones, and cut by flints, and stung by nettles, and torn by briars; who limped and shivered, and glared and growled; and whose teeth chattered in his head as he seized me by the chin.

'O! Don't cut my throat, sir,' I pleaded in terror. 'Pray don't do it, sir.'

'Tell us your name!' said the man. 'Quick!'

'Pip, sir.'

'Once more,' said the man, staring at me. 'Give it mouth!'

'Pip. Pip, sir.'

'Show us where you live,' said the man. 'Pint out the place!'

I pointed to where our village lay, on the flat in-shore among the alder-trees and pollards, a mile or more from the church.

The man, after looking at me for a moment, turned me upside down, and emptied my pockets. There was nothing in them but a piece of bread. When the church came to itself – for he was so sudden and strong that he made it go head over heels before me, and I saw the steeple under my feet – when the church came to itself, I say, I was seated on a high tombstone, trembling, while he ate the bread ravenously.

'You young dog,' said the man, licking his lips, 'what fat cheeks you ha' got.'

I believe they were fat, though I was at that time undersized, for my years, and not strong.

'Darn me if I couldn't eat 'em,' said the man, with a threatening shake of his head, 'and if I han't half a mind to't!'

I earnestly expressed my hope that he wouldn't, and held tighter to the tombstone on which he had put me; partly, to keep myself upon it; partly, to keep myself from crying.

'Now lookee here!' said the man. 'Where's your mother?'

'There, sir!' said I.

He started, made a short run, and stopped and looked over his shoulder.

Persuade, argue, advise: English literary heritage

Worksheet 54b

Great Expectations by Charles Dickens (2)

'There, sir!' I timidly explained. 'Also Georgiana. That's my mother.'

'Oh!' said he, coming back. 'And is that your father alonger your mother?'

'Yes, sir,' said I; 'him too; late of this parish.'

'Ha!' he muttered then, considering. 'Who d'ye live with – supposin' you're kindly let to live, which I han't made up my mind about?'

'My sister, sir – Mrs. Joe Gargery – wife of Joe Gargery, the blacksmith, sir.'

'Blacksmith, eh?' said he. And looked down at his leg.

After darkly looking at his leg and at me several times, he came closer to my tombstone, took me by both arms, and tilted me back as far as he could hold me; so that his eyes looked most powerfully down into mine, and mine looked most helplessly up into his.

'Now lookee here,' he said, 'the question being whether you're to be let to live. You know what a file is?'

'Yes, sir.'

'And you know what wittles[1] is?'

'Yes, sir.'

After each question he tilted me over a little more, so as to give me a greater sense of helplessness and danger.

'You get me a file.' He tilted me again. 'And you get me wittles.' He tilted me again. 'You bring 'em both to me.' He tilted me again. 'Or I'll have your heart and liver out.' He tilted me again.

I was dreadfully frightened, and so giddy that I clung to him with both hands, and said, 'If you would kindly please to let me keep upright, sir, perhaps I shouldn't be sick, and perhaps I could attend more.'

He gave me a most tremendous dip and roll, so that the church jumped over its own weather-cock. Then, he held me by the arms in an upright position on the top of the stone, and went on in these fearful terms:

'You bring me, to-morrow morning early, that file and them wittles. You bring the lot to me, at that old Battery over yonder. You do it, and you never dare to say a word or dare to make a sign concerning your having seen such a person as me, or any person sumever, and you shall be let to live. You fail, or you go from my words in any partickler, no matter how small it is, and your heart and your liver shall be tore out, roasted and ate. Now, I ain't alone, as you may think I am. There's a young man hid with me, in comparison with which young man I am a Angel. That young man hears the words I speak. That young man has a secret way pecooliar to himself, of getting at a boy, and at his heart, and at his liver. It is in wain[2] for a boy to attempt to hide himself from that young man. A boy may lock his door, may be warm in bed, may tuck himself up, may draw the clothes over his head, may think himself comfortable and safe, but that young man will softly creep and creep his way to him and tear him open. I am a keeping that young man from harming of you at the present moment, with great difficulty. I find it wery hard to hold that young man off of your inside. Now, what do you say?'

I said that I would get him the file, and I would get him what broken bits of food I could, and I would come to him at the Battery, early in the morning.

'Say, Lord strike you dead if you don't!' said the man.

I said so, and he took me down.

'Now,' he pursued, 'you remember what you've undertook, and you remember that young man, and you get home!'

[1] *the convict's way of pronouncing 'victuals', an old English term for food*   [2] *in vain, useless*

Persuade, argue, advise: English literary heritage

Worksheet **54c**

Great Expectations
by Charles Dickens (3)

Name
Form

'Goo-good night, sir,' I faltered.

'Much of that!' said he, glancing about him over the cold wet flat. 'I wish I was a frog. Or a eel!'

At the same time, he hugged his shuddering body in both his arms – clasping himself, as if to hold himself together – and limped towards the low church wall. As I saw him go, picking his way among the nettles, and among the brambles that bound the green mounds, he looked in my young eyes as if he were eluding the hands of the dead people, stretching up cautiously out of their graves, to get a twist upon his ankle and pull him in.

When he came to the low church wall, he got over it, like a man whose legs were numbed and stiff, and then turned round to look for me. When I saw him turning, I set my face towards home, and made the best use of my legs. But presently I looked over my shoulder, and saw him going on again towards the river, still hugging himself in both arms, and picking his way with his sore feet among the great stones dropped into the marshes here and there, for stepping-places when the rains were heavy, or the tide was in.

The marshes were just a long black horizontal line then, as I stopped to look after him; and the river was just another horizontal line, not nearly so broad nor yet so black; and the sky was just a row of long angry red lines and dense black lines intermixed. On the edge of the river I could faintly make out the only two black things in all the prospect that seemed to be standing upright; one of these was the beacon by which the sailors steered – like an unhooped cask upon a pole – an ugly thing when you were near it; the other a gibbet,[1] with some chains hanging to it which had once held a pirate. The man was limping on towards this latter, as if he were the pirate come to life, and come down, and going back to hook himself up again. It gave me a terrible turn when I thought so; and as I saw the cattle lifting their heads to gaze after him, I wondered whether they thought so too. I looked all round for the horrible young man, and could see no signs of him. But now I was frightened again, and ran home without stopping.

[1] *gallows*

Persuade, argue, advise: English literary heritage

Worksheet 55

Great Expectations structure cards
pg 69

Pip introduces himself and his family by describing the image he had of his parents and brothers from a picture in his mind based on their tombs.

The convict threatens Pip to persuade him to bring him food and a file. The convict therefore turns Pip upside down again.

Pip describes the landscape around where he lives, including the bleakness of local churchyard (the setting for his earliest significant memory).

The convict adds to Pip's terror by saying that if he doesn't bring him what he wants, his hidden companion, the young man, will tear out his heart and liver and roast and eat them.

The convict threatens Pip – followed by description of the convict.

Pip agrees to bring the convict what he wants the next morning.

The convict demands Pip's name, turns Pip upside down and threatens to eat him.

Pip watches the convict limp away through a landscape that seems to be trying to entrap him.

Pip explains to the convict where his mother is and where he lives.

The setting is described again, including a gibbet which sets Pip's mind racing. The cows too are staring at the convict. Pip runs home.

Persuade, argue, advise: English literary heritage — Worksheet 56

Turning a novel into a film

Name:
Form:

A

1 What problems may face a producer when converting a famous novel into a film? List three key points.
-
-
-

2 What possible advantages may films have over novels? List three key points.
-
-
-

3 What particular problems would face any film-maker in recreating the opening scene of *Great Expectations*? List three key points.
-
-
-

B

Bearing in mind the particular film version of *Great Expectations* that you have seen, answer the following questions in note form:

1 Has the film created a sense of a narrator looking back on his early childhood?

2 Has the film helped the viewer to see the world through the eyes of the young Pip?

3 Was the arrival of the convict scary? If so, what elements helped create this?

4 Does the film make you feel in any way sorry for the convict?

5 Is the way the convict introduces the 'young man' scary? If so, what elements helped create this?

6 What image of the convict are you left with by the end of the scene?

7 What are the key differences between Dickens' opening to *Great Expectations* and the film version?

8 What aspects make the film version effective or not?

9 Has the film-maker done a good job of recreating the essence of the opening scene?

Persuade, argue, advise: English literary heritage — Worksheet 57

Poetic terms (pg 72)

Imagery	Sound effect	Structure of poem
simile	alliteration	sonnet
metaphor	assonance	ballad
symbolism	onomatopoeia	verse
figurative language	rhythm	stanza
conceit	repetition	free verse
personification	rhyme	haiku
powerful vocabulary	metre	word order
	stress	

'The Rime of the Ancient Mariner' by Samuel Taylor Coleridge

Part II

The Sun now rose upon the right:
Out of the sea came he,
Still hid in mist, and on the left
Went down into the sea.

And the good south wind still blew behind,
But no sweet bird did follow,
Nor any day for food and play
Came to the mariners' hollo!

And I had done a hellish thing,
And it would work 'em woe:
For all averred,[1] I had killed the bird
That made the breeze to blow.
Ah wretch! said they, the bird to slay,
That made the breeze to blow!

Nor dim nor red, like God's own head,
The glorious Sun uprist:
Then all averred, I had killed the bird
That brought the fog and mist.
'Twas right, said they, such birds to slay,
That bring the fog and mist.

The fair breeze blew, the white foam flew,
The furrow followed free;
We were the first that ever burst
Into that silent sea.

Down dropt the breeze, the sails dropt down,
'Twas sad as sad could be;
And we did speak only to break
The silence of the sea!

All in a hot and copper sky,
The bloody Sun, at noon,
Right up above the mast did stand,
No bigger than the Moon.

Day after day, day after day,
We stuck, nor breath nor motion;
As idle as a painted ship
Upon a painted ocean.

Water, water, every where,
And all the boards did shrink;
Water, water, every where,
Nor any drop to drink.

The very deep did rot: O Christ!
That ever this should be!
Yea, slimy things did crawl with legs
Upon the slimy sea.

About, about, in reel and rout,
The death-fires danced at night;
The water, like a witch's oils,
Burnt green, and blue and white.

And some in dreams assured were
Of the Spirit that plagued us so;
Nine fathom deep he had followed us
From the land of mist and snow.

And every tongue, through utter drought,
Was withered at the root;
We could not speak, no more than if
We had been choked with soot.

Ah! well-a-day! what evil looks
Had I from old and young!
Instead of the cross, the Albatross
About my neck was hung.

[1] *claimed, stated definitely*

Persuade, argue, advise: Campaign literature — Worksheet 59

Amusing Ourselves to Death
by Neil Postman

Name
Form

Reach Out and Elect Someone

1 In *The Last Hurrah*, Edwin O'Connor's fine novel about lusty party politics in Boston, Mayor Frank Skeffington tries to instruct his young nephew in the realities of political machinery. Politics, he tells him, is the greatest spectator sport in America. In 1966, Ronald Reagan[1] used a different metaphor. 'Politics,' he said, 'is just like show business.'

2 Although sports has now become a major branch of show business, it still contains elements that make Skeffington's vision of politics somewhat more encouraging than Reagan's. In any sport the standard of excellence is well known to both the players and the spectators, and an athlete's reputation rises and falls by his or her proximity to that standard. Where an athlete stands in relation to it cannot easily be disguised or faked, which means that David Garth[2] can do very little to improve the image of an outfielder with a .218 batting average. It also means that a public opinion poll on the question, Who is the best woman tennis player in the world?, is meaningless. The public's opinion has nothing to do with it. Martina Navratilova's[3] serve provides the decisive answer.

3 One may also note that spectators at a sporting event are usually well aware of the rules of the game and the meaning of each piece of the action. There is no way for a batter who strikes out with the bases loaded[4] to argue the spectators into believing that he has done a useful thing. If politics were like a sporting event, there would be several virtues to attach to its name: clarity, honesty, excellence.

4 But what virtues attach to politics if Ronald Reagan is right? Show business is not entirely without an idea of excellence, but its main business is to please the crowd, and its principal instrument is artifice.[5] If politics is like show business, then the idea is not to pursue excellence, clarity or honesty but to *appear* as if you are, which is another matter altogether. And what the other matter is can be expressed in one word: advertising.

---

[1] *Ronald Reagan was a radio sports commentator turned 'B' movie actor who was the American president from 1980 to 1988*
[2] *David Garth was an American sports reporter who particularly focused on baseball in which a .218 batting average is very poor*
[3] *Martina Navratilova dominated women's tennis for many years in the 1980s and 1990s*
[4] *describes the situation where a baseball player, through mis-hitting, ruins a great opportunity to score themselves and get three other batters home*
[5] *crafty or subtle deception*

Persuade, argue, advise: Campaign literature

Worksheet 60a

Election manifestos (1)

Name:
Form:

Conservative Party

It's time for a Government that will deliver

IT'S time for a Government that will deliver.

It's time to support marriage and the family; time for a war on crime; time to cut taxes and regulation; time for our schools and hospitals to benefit from choice and freedom; time to show respect to our pensioners; time for real savings not welfare dependency; time to endow our universities; time to rebuild our inner cities; time to end the crisis in the countryside; time to be in Europe, but not run by it.

It's time for common sense.

Time for common sense in Scotland

We are determined that once again there will be a substantial body of Scottish Conservative MPs in the House of Commons. At present the left of centre parties have a monopoly of the Scottish seats in Parliament. This is unhealthy for Scotland, bad for Scottish business and industry, and harmful to the promotion of free enterprise, low taxation, home ownership and personal responsibility.

Time for common sense in Wales

William Hague has a vision of a strong and proud nation, governed by common sense policies, which are right for Wales and right for Britain. Under him, Wales will grow stronger and its public services will improve.

Wales cannot afford another term of a Labour government that has done so much damage. It's time for common sense.

William Hague

Labour Party

Your family – the family manifesto

MORE doctors ... more teachers ... more police ... more nurses

This election is about the choice facing your family. Whether to move forward – to build on the lower mortgages, low inflation, the extra money going into our schools and hospitals. Or whether to tear up that progress and go back to the bad days of boom and bust, 15 per cent interest rates and public services starved of cash.

Families will get extra help, with up to £1,000 Children's Tax Credit for the under-ones. Pensioners will get a winter fuel payment every year, and there will be more doctors, nurses, teachers and police to reform our public services. But if our opponents get their way none of this would happen.

I believe that families need all the help we can give them, to balance the growing pressures of work and family life. We have put in place the foundations, but I know how much we still need to do. With your support, your family, all Britain's families, can take the next big steps forward.

Tony Blair

Persuade, argue, advise: Campaign literature

Worksheet 60b

Election manifestos (2)

Liberal Democrat Party

A Real Chance for Real Change

Freedom
Justice
Honesty

Three simple words. Freedom, justice, honesty. These sum up what the Liberal Democrats stand for.

Freedom – because everybody should have the opportunity to make the most of their life. **Justice** – because freedom depends on fairness.

Honesty – because where fairness has a cost, like investing in schools, hospitals and pensions, we explain how it will be paid for.

This manifesto sets out our priorities: investing in schools and hospitals to cut class sizes and waiting times; extra police to prevent crime and catch criminals; increasing the basic state pension; and providing free personal care.

In Scotland, where Liberal Democrats are part of the government, we have already guaranteed free personal care. We have also abolished tuition fees, and we want to do this for the rest of the United Kingdom.

We will also recognise the professionalism of teachers, doctors, nurses and the police, valuing their contribution to the community. We believe that they must be given the freedom to exercise their professional judgement.

All our policies have a green dimension. So there is an environmental section in every chapter, a green thread binding together all our thinking. Without steps to preserve our planet for future generations, none of our other policies would have much purpose.

Charles Kennedy MP

Persuade, argue, advise: Campaign literature

Worksheet 61

Rhetorical devices analysis grid

pg 75

Name:
Form:

Device	Evidence
Repetition	
Personal approach from party leader using 'I' and 'we'	
Short paragraphs	
Sound bites/slogan	
Linking by repetition rather than logic	
Direct appeal to reader – 'you'/'yours'	
Simple short sentences	
No complex vocabulary	
Claims that sound impressive but don't actually mean very much	
Very little, if any, use of evidence	
Emotive language	
Lines that sound as if they could be from a fairy story	
Lines that could be from advertising	

Labour / Conservative / Liberal Democrat (highlight the party you are focusing on)

English Frameworking 3: Teacher's Resources © HarperCollins Publishers 2002

Persuade, argue, advise: Campaign literature

Worksheet 62

Election briefing from *The Week*, 2 June 2001

Name
Form

How the parties differ over ... crime

The Tories have sought to make crime a central election issue by devoting the first broadcast of the campaign to an attack on the Government's scheme for the early release of prisoners. Is a tougher line on crime likely to prove effective with the electorate?

Is crime an important electoral issue?

According to a Mori poll in *The Economist*, it's the third most important matter on the electorate's mind. Forty-four per cent cited it as a very important issue that would help determine their voting choice. Only education (53%) and healthcare (61%) ranked higher among voter concerns.

Have crime levels been rising, as the Tories say?

Probably not. The British Crime Survey – the most reliable guide to levels of crime – shows that almost all categories of crime, having risen consistently for two decades, have fallen since the mid-nineties. This has less to do with policy than with demographics.[1] The age group responsible for most criminal offences is 16 to 25-year-olds, and the recent decline in their number is by and large mirrored in an improvement in car and home security. There are two exceptions. Over the past year there have been sudden upsurges in robbery (up by 21%) and violent attacks (up 8%). But if young men hitting each other after they have had a drink are excluded from the violent crime figures, the picture seems less bleak. As for the upsurge in robberies, this is almost entirely due to a new and hitherto unrecorded crime: mobile phone thefts by younger teenagers.

So is concern over British crime levels misplaced?

Not if we make comparison with other countries. Research over the past year shows that people in England and Wales are more likely to be the victims of crime than the citizens of almost any other industrialised nation. The British, according to the international survey, are at greater risk than any other nationality of having their car stolen. And with the exception of Australians, they are also at greater risk of being assaulted, robbed, sexually attacked and having their homes burgled.

What do the parties propose to do about it?

Responding to public pressure, all parties are promising tougher sentences, though the Lib Dems also have a strong line on crime prevention and urge greater use of electronic tagging, fines, reparation to victims and probation orders. Labour promises to introduce tougher sentences for persistent offenders and to create more than 3,000 additional high-security prison and hospital places. The Tories want to increase tenfold the number of places at secure training centres for persistent young offenders and give police new powers to crack down on drug dealers, with tougher penalties for those convicted. They also insist that any prison term handed down by the courts should be the actual term served, and plan to abolish Labour's Early Release Scheme.

But do tougher sentences work?

The Tories have sought to capitalise on the unpopularity of Labour's scheme by claiming that of the 34,911 offenders given early release, 1,095 have committed crimes while under 'home curfew'. However, more than 95% successfully completed the scheme; and only 9% of those released early re-offended within six months of getting out, compared with fully 40% of those who were not released early. Locking people up for longer is also extremely expensive. The Tories' plans for tougher sentencing would increase the prison population by a fifth, costing an extra £588m. Labour's proposals would have similar consequences. Britain already has one of the higher prison populations in Europe, with 125 prisoners for every 100,000 members of the population, compared with 90 in France and 95 in Germany. (In the USA the figure is 680 per 100,000.)

What other solutions do the parties offer?

All of them intone the same mantra[2]: put more bobbies on the beat. Labour say they would recruit 6,000 more police officers, as do the Lib Dems, who also want a further 2,000 part-time 'community officers'. The Tories have pledged to increase numbers by reversing cuts made under Labour.

---

[1] *population statistics*
[2] *endlessly repeat the same sound*

Persuade, argue, advise: Campaign literature

Worksheet 63a

Conservative Party's manifesto on crime

Name

Form

Time for common sense

Through our lives

Living safely

Common sense means having enough police to keep our streets safe and a criminal justice system that reflects our values rather than undermines them

- Increase police numbers
- Free police from bureaucracy so that they can get on with policing
- Take persistent young offenders off our streets
- Criminals to serve the sentence given by the court
- More rights for victims

We may have grown more prosperous as a nation, but the quality of our life is still impoverished by crime.

Decent people, who work hard and who obey the law, are outraged that criminals seem free to make their lives a misery.

Labour have talked tough on law and order but they have failed to deliver. Police numbers have fallen, and violent crime is on the rise.

It's time for common sense.

Conservatives will trust the instincts of the mainstream majority on law and order. That means more police and less bureaucracy holding them back. It also means tougher sentences for some crimes and more honest sentencing for all crimes.

> "It's time to stop turning a blind eye to crimes committed by young offenders and ensure instead that they are put back on the right track."

More police, tougher sentences

Conservatives will increase the number of police officers on our streets by reversing the cuts in police numbers that Labour have made.

English Frameworking 3: Teacher's Resources © HarperCollins*Publishers* 2002

Persuade, argue, advise: Campaign literature

Worksheet 63b

Labour Party's manifesto on crime

Name
Form

Tough on crime
Tough on the causes of crime

Improving the quality of life for everyone means we must tackle crime and the fear of crime. It's why Labour promised to be tough on crime and the causes of crime.

With Labour, falling unemployment, better education and tougher action against truancy are helping tackle some of the causes of crime. And we've also put in place the most co-ordinated attack on crime for a generation.

The police are in the frontline of any anti-crime strategy. Police numbers are rising. Already we have funded 3,000 extra police recruits, and the extra investment we are putting in should provide 6,000 more recruits, to raise police numbers to their highest ever level.

The efforts of the police will be backed by the courts. We will reform sentencing so that persistent offenders get tougher sentences, as well as expanding drugs treatment. The youth justice system has been overhauled to cut delays. Spending on CCTV cameras has increased four-fold.

Drugs drive crime. Sentences for drug dealers have been increased. We will confiscate the proceeds of crime to hit the crime barons. Compulsory drugs testing is in place for prisoners, plus a new emphasis on rehabilitation.

But crime is still too high – especially violent crime. The dramatic falls in burglary and car crime over the last four years show how targeting resources and police time works.

Persuade, argue, advise: Campaign literature

Worksheet 63c

Liberal Democrat Party's manifesto on crime

Name

Form

Law and Order

We all want freedom from crime. Fear of crime blights the lives of many people, particularly the most vulnerable in society. The state should offer all its citizens equal and adequate protection.

Our approach is rooted in the belief that the best way to beat crime in the medium and long term is to have effective policies to tackle its causes.

Liberal Democrats will:

- Recruit 6000 extra police officers
- Fund 2000 part-time community officers
- Reinforce front-line police with a new Community Safety Force and by retaining retired officers in a back-up role
- Cut reoffending by preparing prisoners adequately for a law-abiding life on their release
- Give victims greater rights to be heard in court

During their eighteen years in office, the Conservatives pursued a policy on crime which was superficially populist yet highly ineffective. They filled the prisons to overflowing, at a huge cost to the taxpayer. Crime doubled, violent crime rose year after year, and the number of convictions fell. Meanwhile, contrary to repeated promises, police numbers fell during the last Conservative government.

Labour has been trying to sound as tough, or tougher, than the Conservatives, but is no more effective. Police numbers have fallen further over the past four years. Labour too often proposes simplistic solutions. Many are impractical or irrelevant. Some actually undermine civil liberties.

Persuade, argue, advise: Campaign literature — Worksheet 64

Crime analysis grid

Labour / Conservative / Lib Dem policy on crime *(highlight the party you are focusing on)*	
Bias: 3 examples	★
	★
	★
Key arguments	★
	★
	★
Key points of policy	★
	★
	★

Persuade, argue, advise: Campaign literature — Worksheet 65

Letter to the editor

SIR – It's interesting to read the bleatings of your commentators and correspondents about apathy¹ in the run-up to the general election, when everywhere you look there are people champing at the bit to have their say and do their bit: from the anti-capitalist demonstrators in London to the woman who harangued² Tony Blair outside the hospital in Birmingham.

More worryingly, we have recently had the Portsmouth anti-paedophile³ vigilantes⁴ taking their own highly effective action to achieve results, the fuel protesters grinding Britain to a halt, and the blessed farmers dictating to the Government, as the electorate (or non-electorate as many fear we are now becoming) realise that People Power can do what a vote in a ballot-box cannot.

We need a Senator Jeffords effect,⁵ where a thoughtful and articulate⁶ politician can create change and force his leader to rethink certain key decisions and reflect the public mood (the best news from America in four months); because it is our politicians who are apathetic, not us. They need to wise up and engage the voters, not the media, in the debate, or the most motivated of us will gang up and get our own way anyway, whichever truckload of old bores gets in.

SJ Bentley

---

¹ *lack of interest or feeling, indifference*
² *spoke angrily to*
³ *adult who is sexually attracted by young children*
⁴ *self-appointed protector of public order*
⁵ *President Bush in America had a majority of one in the House of Representatives. Senator Jeffords, a member of the Bush administration, decided to resign on a point of principle thus significantly limiting Bush's power*
⁶ *able to speak fluently and coherently*

Liza's first appearance in London society (*Pygmalion*, Act 3) (1)

Higgins eventually agrees to teach Liza how to 'speak beautifully', boasting to his friend Pickering that 'in three months I could pass that girl off as a duchess at an ambassador's garden party'. In Act 3 Higgins is ready to show Liza off to his mother, who is sitting in the drawing room of her elegant Chelsea flat, when the well-to-do Eynsford Hill family unexpectedly call.

	THE PARLORMAID	(*opening the door*) Miss Doolittle. (*She withdraws.*)
	HIGGINS	(*rising hastily and running to Mrs Higgins*) Here she is, mother. (*He stands on tiptoe and makes signs over his mother's head to Liza to indicate to her which lady is her hostess.*)
5		*Liza, who is exquisitely dressed, produces an impression of such remarkable distinction and beauty as she enters that they all rise, quite fluttered. Guided by Higgins's signals, she comes to Mrs Higgins with studied grace.*
	LIZA	(*speaking with* pedantic[1] *correctness of pronunciation and great beauty of tone*) How do you do, Mrs Higgins? (*She gasps slightly in making sure of the H in Higgins, but is quite successful.*) Mr Higgins told me I might come.
10	MRS HIGGINS	(*cordially*) Quite right: I'm very glad indeed to see you.
	PICKERING	How do you do, Miss Doolittle?
	LIZA	(*shaking hands with him*) Colonel Pickering, is it not?
	MRS EYNSFORD HILL	I feel sure we have met before, Miss Doolittle. I remember your eyes.
15	LIZA	How do you do? (*She sits down on the* ottoman[2] *gracefully in the place just left vacant by Higgins.*)
	MRS EYNSFORD HILL	(*introducing*) My daughter Clara.
	LIZA	How do you do?
	CLARA	(*impulsively*) How do you do? (*She sits down on the ottoman beside Liza,*
20		*devouring her with her eyes.*)
	FREDDY	(*coming to their side of the ottoman*) I've certainly had the pleasure.
	MRS EYNSFORD HILL	(*introducing*) My son Freddy.
	LIZA	How do you do? (*Freddy bows and sits down in the Elizabethan chair, infatuated.*)
	HIGGINS	(*suddenly*) By George, yes: it all comes back to me! (*They stare at him.*) Covent
25		Garden! (*Lamentably*[3]) What a damned thing!
	MRS HIGGINS	Henry, please! (*He is about to sit on the edge of the table.*) Don't sit on my writing table: you'll break it.
	HIGGINS	(*sulkily*) Sorry.

He goes to the divan,[4] *stumbling into the fender and over the fire-irons on his way; extricating himself*
30 *with muttered* imprecations;[5] *and finishing his disastrous journey by throwing himself so impatiently on the divan that he almost breaks it. Mrs Higgins looks at him, but controls herself and says nothing. A long and painful pause ensues.*

	MRS HIGGINS	(*at last, conversationally*) Will it rain, do you think?
	LIZA	The shallow depression in the west of these islands is likely to move slowly in an
35		easterly direction. There are no indications of any great change in the barometrical situation.
	FREDDY	Ha! ha! how awfully funny!
	LIZA	What is wrong with that, young man? I bet I got it right.
	FREDDY	Killing!

[1] *over-careful*   [2] *chair*   [3] *distressed*   [4] *sofa*   [5] *curses*

Analyse, review, comment: Playscripts — Worksheet **66b**

Liza's first appearance in London society (*Pygmalion*, Act 3) (2)

Name:
Form:

40	MRS EYNSFORD HILL	I'm sure I hope it won't turn cold. There's so much influenza about. It runs right through our whole family regularly every spring.
	LIZA	(*darkly*) My aunt died of influenza: so they said.
	MRS EYNSFORD HILL	(*clicks her tongue sympathetically*) !!!
	LIZA	(*in the same tragic tone*) But it's my belief they done the old woman in.
45	MRS HIGGINS	(*puzzled*) Done her in?
	LIZA	Y-e-e-e-es, Lord love you! Why should she die of influenza? She come through diphtheria[1] right enough the year before. I saw her with my own eyes. Fairly blue with it, she was. They all thought she was dead; but my father he kept ladling gin down her throat til she came to so sudden that she bit the bowl off the spoon.
50	MRS EYNSFORD HILL	(*startled*) Dear me!
	LIZA	(*piling up the indictment[2]*) What call would a woman with that strength in her have to die of influenza? What become of her new straw hat that should have come to me? Somebody pinched it; and what I say is, them as pinched it done her in.
	MRS EYNSFORD HILL	What does doing her in mean?
55	HIGGINS	(*hastily*) Oh, that's the new small talk. To do a person in means to kill them.
	MRS EYNSFORD HILL	(*to Liza, horrified*) You surely don't believe that your aunt was killed?
	LIZA	Do I not! Them she lived with would have killed her for a hat-pin, let alone a hat.
	MRS EYNSFORD HILL	But it can't have been right for your father to pour spirits down her throat like that. It might have killed her.
60	LIZA	Not her. Gin was mother's milk to her. Besides, he'd poured so much down his own throat that he knew the good of it.
	MRS EYNSFORD HILL	Do you mean that he drank?
	LIZA	Drank! My word! Something chronic.
	MRS EYNSFORD HILL	How dreadful for you!
65	LIZA	Not a bit. It never did him no harm what I could see. But then he did not keep it up regular. (*Cheerfully*) On the burst, as you might say, from time to time. And always more agreeable when he had a drop in … (*To Freddy, who is in convulsions of suppressed laughter*) Here! What are you sniggering at?
	FREDDY	The new small talk. You do it so awfully well.
70	LIZA	If I was doing it proper, what was you laughing at? (*To Higgins*) Have I said anything I oughtn't?
	MRS HIGGINS	(*interposing*) Not at all, Miss Doolittle.
	LIZA	Well, that's a mercy, anyhow. (*Expansively*) What I always say is –
	HIGGINS	(*rising and looking at his watch*) Ahem!
75	LIZA	(*looking round at him; taking the hint; and rising*) Well: I must go. (*They all rise. Freddy goes to the door.*) So pleased to have met you. Goodbye. (*She shakes hands with Mrs Higgins.*)
	MRS HIGGINS	Goodbye.
	LIZA	Goodbye, Colonel Pickering.
80	PICKERING	Goodbye, Miss Doolittle. (*They shake hands.*)
	LIZA	(*nodding to the others*) Goodbye, all.
	FREDDY	(*opening the door for her*) Are you walking across the Park, Miss Doolittle? If so –
	LIZA	(*perfectly elegant diction[3]*) Walk! Not bloody likely. (*Sensation*) I am going in a taxi. (*She goes out.*)

[1] *a disease*   [2] *accusation*   [3] *pronunciation*

English Frameworking 3: Teacher's Resources   © HarperCollinsPublishers 2002

Analyse, review, comment: Playscripts

Worksheet 67

Revealing the subtext

Said	Thought
I'm sorry to waste your time, doctor	I'm really worried about the pains I'm getting behind my eyes
We had such a brilliant holiday	Actually it rained every day and my parents argued
Thank you for the money you sent me, Gran	It'll just about cover the cost of this phone call
Sam seems really nice	What awful taste s/he's got in boy/girlfriends
Can I check to see if you got your homework right?	I may be able to copy it
Thankyou for taking the trouble of coming to see me	I could do without this anxious parent in my office – I've got a school to run
Yeah, my dad earns loads of money too	Actually he's just been made redundant
Yes, I'd love to come to the cinema	But not with you

Analyse, review, comment: Playscripts

Worksheet 68a

Dramatic irony in Sheridan's *The Rivals* (1)

Name
Form

Lydia Languish wants to marry for love not money, so the rich Captain Absolute disguises himself as Ensign Beverley, a poor army officer, and wins her love. Lydia's aunt and guardian, Mrs Malaprop, insists that she marries Captain Absolute, and forbids her from seeing Beverley, not realizing they are the same person. Beverley and Lydia write to each other secretly, but Mrs Malaprop has uncovered one of their letters …

	MRS MALAPROP	You are not ignorant, captain, that this giddy girl has somehow contrived to fix her affections on a beggarly, strolling, eaves-dropping ensign, whom none of us have seen, and nobody knows anything of.
5	CAPTAIN ABSOLUTE	Oh, I have heard the silly affair before. – I'm not at all prejudiced against her on that account.
	MRS MALAPROP	You are very good and very considerate, captain. I am sure I have done everything in my power since I exploded the affair; long ago I laid my positive conjunctions on her, never to think on the fellow again; – I have since laid Sir Anthony's preposition before her; but, I am sorry to say, she seems resolved to decline every particle that I enjoin¹ her.
10		
	CAPTAIN ABSOLUTE	It must be very distressing, indeed, ma'am.
15	MRS MALAPROP	Oh! it gives me the hydrostatics to such a degree. – I thought she had persisted from corresponding with him; but behold, this very day, I have interceded another letter from the fellow; I believe I have it in my pocket.
20	CAPTAIN ABSOLUTE	(*aside*) Oh, the devil! my last note.
	MRS MALAPROP	Ay, here it is.
	CAPTAIN ABSOLUTE	(*aside*) Ay, my note indeed!
	MRS MALAPROP	There, perhaps you may know the writing. (*Gives him the letter.*)
25	CAPTAIN ABSOLUTE	I think I have seen the hand² before – yes, I certainly must have seen this hand before –
	MRS MALAPROP	Nay, but read it, captain.
	CAPTAIN ABSOLUTE	(*reads*) *My soul's idol, my adored Lydia!* Very tender, indeed!
30	MRS MALAPROP	Tender, ay, and profane³ too, o' my conscience!
	CAPTAIN ABSOLUTE	(*reads*) *I am excessively alarmed at the intelligence you send me, the more so as my new rival* –
	MRS MALAPROP	That's you, sir.
35	CAPTAIN ABSOLUTE	(*reads*) *Has universally the character of being an accomplished gentleman, and a man of honour.* – Well, that's handsome enough.
	MRS MALAPROP	Oh, the fellow has some design in writing so.
	CAPTAIN ABSOLUTE	That he had, I'll answer for him, ma'am.

¹ *command* ² *handwriting* ³ *vulgar, disgraceful*

Analyse, review, comment: Playscripts

Worksheet **68b**

Dramatic irony in Sheridan's *The Rivals* (2)

Name
Form

	MRS MALAPROP	But go on, sir – you'll see presently.
40	CAPTAIN ABSOLUTE	(*reads*) *As for the old weather-beaten she-dragon who guards you* – Who can he mean by that?
	MRS MALAPROP	Me, sir! – me! – he means me! – There – what do you think now? – but go on a little further.
45	CAPTAIN ABSOLUTE	Impudent scoundrel! – (*reads*) *I will <u>elude her vigilance</u>,¹ as I am told that the same ridiculous vanity, which makes her dress up her coarse features, and <u>deck</u>² her dull chat with hard words which she don't understand* –
50	MRS MALAPROP	There, sir! an attack upon my language! what do you think of that? – an aspersion upon my parts of speech! was ever such a brute! Sure if I reprehend anything in this world it is the use of my oracular tongue, and a nice derangement of epitaphs!
	CAPTAIN ABSOLUTE	He deserves to be hanged and quartered! let me see – (*reads*) *same ridiculous vanity* –
55	MRS MALAPROP	You need not read it again, sir.
60	CAPTAIN ABSOLUTE	I beg pardon, ma'am – (*reads*) *does also lay her open to the grossest deceptions from flattery and pretended admiration* – an impudent coxcomb! – *so that I have a scheme to see you shortly with the old <u>harridan's</u>³ consent, and even to make her a go-between in our interview.* – Was ever such <u>assurance</u>!⁴
	MRS MALAPROP	Did you ever hear anything like it? – he'll elude my vigilance, will he? – Yes, yes! ha! ha! he's very likely to enter these doors; – we'll try who can plot best!
65	CAPTAIN ABSOLUTE	So we will, ma'am – so we will! Ha! ha! ha! a conceited puppy, ha! ha! ha! – Well, but, Mrs Malaprop, as the girl seems so infatuated by this fellow, suppose you were to <u>wink at</u>⁵ her corresponding with him for a little time – let her even plot an <u>elopement</u>⁶ with him – then do you <u>connive at</u>⁷ her escape – while I, just in the nick, will have the fellow laid by the heels, and fairly contrive to carry her off in his stead.
70	MRS MALAPROP	I am delighted with the scheme; never was anything better perpetrated!

¹ escape her notice
² dress up
³ nag
⁴ impudence
⁵ pretend not to notice
⁶ secret marriage
⁷ encourage

Richard Brinsley Sheridan (1751–1816) was born in Dublin but lived most of his life in London. His satirical comedies *The Rivals* (1775) and *School for Scandal* (1777) were his most successful plays. Sheridan also had a long and distinguished parliamentary career.

Analyse, review, comment: Playscripts — Worksheet 69

Characteristics of Standard and non-Standard English

Standard English	Non-Standard English
It is used for writing and in formal education	It is used mainly orally and in informal contexts
Its form changes very little wherever in the world it is used	It has a huge range of variation in form
It has a wide range of vocabulary and uses	It has a limited range of vocabulary and uses
It can be spoken with any accent	It is generally spoken with a particular accent
It is accepted throughout the English-speaking world	Its use is limited to a distinct group
Its rules are formally set down (in dictionaries and in the rules of grammar)	Its rules are not formally set down, so it cannot be taught and learnt easily

Analyse, review, comment: Playscripts

Worksheet 70a

Our Day Out (1)

Mrs Kay has taken her class onto the beach. Carol, who doesn't want to go home, has wandered off and is standing on a cliff looking out to sea. The teachers eventually notice her absence; they start searching for her and Mr Briggs goes up onto the cliffs.

BRIGGS Carol Chandler! (*Briggs approaches. On seeing her he stops and stands a few yards off.*) Just come here. (*She turns and stares at him.*) Who gave you permission to come up here?

CAROL No-one. (*Turning she dismisses him.*)

5 BRIGGS I'm talking to you, Carol Chandler. (*She continues to ignore his presence.*) Now just listen here, young lady ... (*As he goes to move towards her, she turns on him.*)

CAROL Don't you come near me!

BRIGGS (*taken aback, stopping*) Pardon!

10 CAROL I don't want you to come near me.

BRIGGS Well, in that case just get yourself moving and let's get down to the beach. (*Pause*)

CAROL You go. I'm not coming.

BRIGGS You what?

15 CAROL Tell Mrs Kay that she can go home without me. I'm stoppin' here ... In Wales. (*Pause*)

BRIGGS Now just you listen to me – I've had just about enough today, just about enough, and I'm not putting up with a pile of silliness from the likes of you. Now come on ... (*He starts to move towards her. She takes a step towards*

20 *the edge of the cliff.*)

CAROL Try an' get me an' I'll jump over. (*Briggs stops, astounded. There is an angry pause. She continues to ignore him.*)

BRIGGS Now come on! I'll not tell you again. (*He moves forward. Again, she moves nearer to the edge. He stops and they look at each other.*) I'll give you five

25 seconds. Just five seconds. One ... two ... three ... four ... I'm warning you ... five! (*She stares at him blankly. Briggs stares back in impotent[1] rage.*)

CAROL I've told y' ... I'm not comin' down with y'. (*Pause*) I'll jump y' know ... I will.

BRIGGS Just what are you trying to do to me?

CAROL I've told you. Leave me alone and I won't jump. (*Pause*) I wanna stay here.

30 Where it's nice.

BRIGGS Stay here? How could you stay here? What would you do? Where would you live?

CAROL I'll be alright.

BRIGGS Now I've told you. Stop being so silly.

35 CAROL (*turning on him*) What do you worry for, eh? Eh? You don't care, do y'? Do y'?

BRIGGS What? About you? Listen ... if I didn't care, why am I here, now, trying to stop you doing something stupid?

CAROL Because if I jumped over, you'll get into trouble when you get back to school. That's why, Briggsy! So stop goin' on. You hate me.

[1] *powerless*

Analyse, review, comment: Playscripts

Worksheet 70b

Our Day Out (2)

Name
Form

40	BRIGGS	Don't be ridiculous – just because I'm a schoolteacher it doesn't mean to say that …
	CAROL	Don't lie, you! I know you hate me. I've seen you goin' home in your car, passin' us on the street. And the way y' look at us. You hate all the kids. (*She turns again to the sea, dismissing him.*)
45	BRIGGS	What … makes you think that? Eh?
	CAROL	Why can't I just stay out here, eh? Why can't I live in one of them nice white houses an' do the garden an' that?
	BRIGGS	Look, Carol … you're talking as though you've given up on life already. You sound as though life for you is just ending, instead of beginning. Now why can't,
50		I mean, if it's what you want, what's to stop you working hard at school from now on, getting a good job and then moving out here when you're old enough? Eh?
	CAROL	(*Turns slowly to look at him. Contempt.*) Don't be friggin' stupid. (*She turns and looks down at the sea below.*) It's been a great day today. I loved it. I don't
55		wanna leave here an' go home. (*She moves to the edge of the cliff. Briggs is alarmed but unable to move.*) If I stayed though, it wouldn't be no good. You'd send the coppers to get me.
	BRIGGS	We'd have to. How would you survive out here?
	CAROL	I know. (*Pause*) I'm not goin' back though.
60	BRIGGS	Please …
	CAROL	Sir, sir, y' know if you'd been my old feller, I woulda been alright, wouldn't I? (*Briggs slowly holds out his hand. She moves to the very edge of the cliff. Briggs is aware of how close she is.*)
	BRIGGS	Carol. Carol, please come away from there. (*stretching out his hand to her*)
65		Please. (*Carol looks at him and a smile breaks across her face.*)
	CAROL	Sir … sir you don't half look funny, y' know.
	BRIGGS	(*smiling back at her*) Why?
	CAROL	Sir, you should smile more often, y' look great when y' smile.
	BRIGGS	Come on, Carol. (*He gingerly[1] approaches her.*)
70	CAROL	What'll happen to me for doin' this, sir?
	BRIGGS	Nothing. I promise you.
	CAROL	Sir, y' promisin' now, but what about when we get back t' school?
	BRIGGS	(*almost next to her now*) It won't even be mentioned.
		(*She turns and looks down at the drop then back at Briggs's outstretched arm. Carol lifts
75		her hand to his. She slips. Briggs grabs out quickly and manages to pull her up to him. Briggs wraps his arm around her.*)

[1] *cautiously*

Willy Russell was born near Liverpool in 1947. He ran a hairdresser's salon before passing exams at night school and training to be a teacher. He started writing plays at the teachers' college and is now one of the most performed English dramatists. Many of his plays have been made into films and musicals, including *Educating Rita* and *Shirley Valentine*. *Our Day Out* was originally written as a television play in 1976; it was adapted for the stage in 1983.

Analyse, review, comment: Playscripts

Worksheet 71

Planning frame for improvisation

Name:
Form:

Fill in the grid below to help you plan your improvisation.

Names of characters plus important features	• • • •
What incident will provoke the crisis that is the focus of your scene?	
How will this crisis lead to a resolution?	
What sort of resolution will it be – a change of action or character, or a new understanding or outlook?	
How will you build up the tension?	
Could you use dramatic irony to increase the tension and impact of the scene?	
How will the dialogue bring out the characters?	
What role will the two minor characters play (Mother and Brother/Sister)? For example, will their actions and/or character reflect on or contrast with the main action?	
What other dramatic techniques will you use?	
How can you end the scene in the most effective way?	

Analyse, review, comment: Playscripts — **Worksheet 72**

Evaluating the performances

Name:
Form:

Fill in the grid below to evaluate the performances of other groups. Put an asterisk against the most successful performance.

	Group 1	Group 2	Group 3	Group 4
Writing • Was the dialogue strong, natural and effective? • Was the script well structured? • Were the minor characters given effective roles? • Did the play include some memorable moments?				
Directing • Was there an overall sense of purpose and direction to the acting? • Was there a build up of tension and a resolution? • Was any use made of dramatic irony or other techniques? • Was the interpretation unusual, imaginative or thought-provoking?				
Acting (Think about all the characters, not just the **protagonists**) • Did they relate naturally to one another? • Did they bring out the real causes of the tension between them? • Did they make good use of expression, tone and gesture? • Did they use the space well?				

protagonist the main character in a play or story

English Frameworking 3: Teacher's Resources © HarperCollins*Publishers* 2002

Analyse, review, comment: Playscripts — Worksheet 73

Evaluating your contribution to drama activities

pg 95

Name:
Form:

	Yes	Sometimes	No
Acting and working in role			
Am I willing to adopt a variety of roles?			
Do I sustain and deepen the roles that I adopt?			
Do I interact effectively with the other characters?			
Can I show the audience my real thoughts?			
Do I make effective use of tone, gesture and movement?			
Scriptwriting and directing			
Can I think of effective and natural dialogue?			
Do I have good ideas about plot and structure?			
Do I have a clear idea of where I want the performance to go?			
Am I able to persuade and encourage others?			
Do I make the best use of all the actors?			
Can I make use of dramatic irony and other techniques?			
Working as a group			
Am I willing to work with everyone in the group?			
Do I help others to get involved in the activities?			
Do I contribute ideas?			
Do I listen to other people's ideas?			
Can I adapt my own ideas in the light of criticism?			

I have developed my drama skills in these three areas:

- ....
- ....
- ....

My targets for increasing my skills further are:

- ....
- ....
- ....

English Frameworking 3: Teacher's Resources © HarperCollins Publishers 2002

Analyse, review, comment: Journalism — Worksheet 74

Levels of formality

Slang	Colloquial	Informal	Formal
Popped his clogs	OK, mate	Crazy	Yours sincerely
Cool, baby	Let's have a drink	Lashings of cream	Can you not see?
You're round the bend	Give us a kiss	Can't	Of unsound mind
That's wicked, man	How y'a doin'?	Get the hang of	Compare and contrast

Analyse, review, comment: Journalism

Worksheet 75

Theatre listings

Surname of playwright only – abbreviated style.

Informal grammar: the dash used simply to add a point. Neither sentence in the entry has a main clause.

Reference to another work by the same playwright to help readers.

THE RIVALS

Salisbury Playhouse
Thursday September 6–Saturday 29
8pm

Sheridan's top quipping Restoration comedy – all mistaken identity and improbable outcomes from the scribbler of School for Scandal. Set in Georgian Bath and featuring the legendary word-mangler Mrs Malaprop.

THE REAL THING

Bristol Old Vic
Friday September 7–Saturday 29
7.30pm

Tom Stoppard honed his gifts for writing at Bristol's very own Evening Post, and his complex prose returns to the city with this revival of his bittersweet comedy about the merging of professional and personal lives for playwright Henry (Neil Pearson from telly's Drop the Dead Donkey). Quality board-treaders Marsha Fitzalan (from The New Statesman) and Geraldine Alexander (who's not really a TV sort of person) complete the line up.

Structure: two simple sentences with no connectives.

Informal vocabulary: also amusing in this context, as contrasts with the mannered play.

Two two-word noun phrases to sum up the play in a snappy way.

Reference to a key (attractive) character to help and entice readers.

Analyse, review, comment: Journalism — **Worksheet 76**

Writing a theatre listing

Name:
Form:

Before you start writing your listings entry, make some brief notes to help you organize your ideas.

• Title	
• Place and time	

Information that you want to include	
• Plot	
• Performance	
• Actors	

Words and phrases that sum up aspects of the performance in a concise and humorous way	
• Plot	
• Performance	
• Actors	

Now write your entry here: remember that it should consist of no more than two sentences.

English Frameworking 3: Teacher's Resources © HarperCollins*Publishers* 2002

Analyse, review, comment: Journalism

Review of *My Fair Lady*

It's still a dream musical – or musical play – with more than a touch of magic about it. I came away from Trevor Nunn's[1] newly minted production of *My Fair Lady* last night marveling at the variety of its seductive music, the lure of its songs, the strength of its emotional appeal. The fascinating, sex-free relationship between Jonathan Pryce's desiccated[2] mother-fixated[3] Professor of Phonetics, Henry Higgins, and Martine McCutcheon's spirited Edwardian flower girl makes other more traditional romances in musicals pale by comparison.

Miss McCutcheon sounds the real thing: she's a boisterous cockney Eliza – more authentic than Julie Andrews or Audrey Hepburn. And once Higgins has pummelled and bullied her voice into upper-class shape, it sounds just right – careful and precarious. McCutcheon social-climbs into high society, statuesque in white, tiara and diamonds, radiating both the jaunty assurance and vulnerability that marks her entire, impressive performance.

At the end, Nunn springs his provocative surprise. Pryce and McCutcheon stand facing each other, elbows folded and smiling inscrutably,[4] as if posed to settle for the joys of living together as passionate friends. The flower girl has won independence in an age when women could not vote and has moulded the middle-aged Professor into an endearing father figure. Higgins, whom Pryce persuasively presents first as a smug, smooth patroniser[5] and later as a little boy lost in middle-age, has been humanised by discovering his capacity to feel for someone as much as for phonetics. Pryce's performance, though lacking Rex Harrison's charisma and air of testy self-absorption, does have a true emotional core.

There are other advantages too. How fresh and radical in its mockery of our class-system and the snobberies of upper-crust England this new *My Fair Lady* looks. The famous choreographer Matthew Bourne who gave us the all-male *Swan Lake* and converted Bizet's *Carmen* into *The Carman*, gives Nunn's production a satirical shot in the vitals for the big scenic spectaculars. Bourne transforms the Ascot scene, with its Gilbert and Sullivan pastiche[6] songs, into a lethally comic dance and parade of the stiff-limbed aristocrats. Dressed in extravagant black, they twitch like sombre marionettes.[7] When McCutcheon's Eliza delightfully tries out her strained new accent, and her small-talk becomes far too lengthy, with the odd phrase all too cockney, they sit in a long line looking daggers.

The Queen of Transylvania's royal ball, with the crop haired, haughty monarchs and the shaven headed Prince bizarrely looking like refugees from the gay night-club Heaven, seems mockingly staged as an event of grand tackiness. Bourne's work is completed in the brilliant pub and music-hall turns for Dennis Waterman's finely pitched, lecherous Alfred Doolitttle, with dustbin-lids attached to the feet of stomping costermonger[8] dancers as they sing "With a little bit of luck" and "I'm getting married in the morning."

Nunn's production keeps the right, snappy pace. The supporting performers are exceptionally supportive. Nicholas Le Prevost's repressed,[9] thoroughly martial Colonel Pickering, Patsy Rowland's bohemian[10] housekeeper, Caroline Blackiston's Mrs Higgins and Mark Umbers as the smitten[11] Freddy, who boasts the company's best singing voice, all match or sometimes surpass their film counterparts. Fairly magical, indeed.

Nicholas de Jongh

---

[1] the director
[2] dry
[3] over-attached to his mother
[4] mysteriously
[5] someone who treats others as children
[6] imitation
[7] puppets
[8] street-seller
[9] not showing his feelings
[10] unconventional
[11] love-struck

Analyse, review, comment: Journalism

The celebrity interview

Victoria Beckham Gets Personal with Tony Parsons

For the last 10 minutes Victoria Beckham has been secretly eyeing up the gigantic fruit bowl that sits between us.

It's quite a fruit bowl – overflowing with mangoes, kiwi fruit, peaches and assorted berries. In the end Victoria's hunger gets the better of her and she snatches up a solitary blackberry, quickly popping it in her mouth.

'Is that your lunch?' I ask.

'No,' she deadpans. 'This is my breakfast.'

Posh in blackberry-for-breakfast shocker? No, Mrs Beckham is just doing what she does all the time. She's kidding, folks. The month before we met at the top of Virgin Records' office, a mind-blowing 451 items appeared in British newspapers about the artist formerly known as Posh Spice.

Four hundred and fifty-one articles! This is an avalanche of publicity that no one has experienced since Princess Diana was centre stage. This week her autobiography, *Learning to Fly*, came out. Next week it's the single, Not Such An Innocent Girl, and in two weeks there's an album, Victoria Beckham.

But you know that people would be obsessed with her anyway. I ask the object of all this attention to sum up her public image. 'Miserable cow, short skirts, high heels, Bond Street,[1] no personality,' she says. 'People think: that bossy cow, she bosses him about. Anyone who's been in our house will tell you that it's completely the other way around. David's definitely the dominating one.'

We think we know her, but we don't know her at all. The butt of a thousand second-rate comedians is a national treasure who has somehow been turned into a national joke. Football crowds chant about her as though she is the Whore of Babylon[2] when she is much closer to Doris Day.[3]

'I have slept with three men in my life,' she says. 'Just three men. I never had boyfriends at school. When everyone else was going to clubs, I was going to ballet classes. I'm faithful to my husband, I am a good mum, a working mum. I don't drink: you will never see pictures of me drunk outside a night-club, doing topless stuff. I do my work and then I come home and spend time with my family. We don't go to celebrity parties. I don't like any of that bollocks.' She might have the morals of Doris Day, but she has the mouth of a sailor.

It's not forgivable, but you can sort of understand why Victoria gets some stick. In an age when even Tom and Nicole and Kate and Jim[4] are heading for the divorce courts, she has what looks like the perfect marriage. Mr and Mrs Beckham are mad about each other.

'I knew from the first time I met David that I wanted to marry him,' she says. 'If David was to ever cheat on me, I think I would die of a broken heart. I probably would. It would kill me.'

Come on, I say. You're only saying that because you have never really had your heart broken.

'I got my heart broken once. Or I thought it was broken at the time. He was a prat really, a complete tosser. He ended up on Blind Date. I never really loved anyone until I met David. When my first fiancé dumped me, I felt like I was dying.'

I bet he's kicking himself now.

'I bet he is!' she laughs. She laughs a lot. But then she's got a lot to laugh about. Saturday night, she was leaving her husband in Manchester, and she started crying like a little kid. She didn't want to leave him. Because the first big love of her life turned out to be the true love of her life. And how often does that happen?

---

[1] a street in London's West End
[2] a symbol of lust and vice
[3] actress of clean-living roles
[4] Tom Cruise, Nicole Kidman, Kate Winslet, Jim Thrippleton

Analyse, review, comment: Journalism

Worksheet 79

Drafting your celebrity interview

pg 101

Name:
Form:

Jot down your thoughts about the following questions. This will help you give your article an effective structure and style.

How can you begin your article in an effective way? Remember that some description of who your celebrity is will be needed early on – if only in a strapline.	
What is the main subject matter of the interview? Will you stick to this in your article or use it as a springboard into different material, such as your interviewee's appearance and behaviour at the interview?	
How much of yourself and your opinions are you going to include in the article? Or will the focus be entirely on your interviewee?	
How much of the article will contain direct quotation from your celebrity? Will you use reported speech for variety?	
Will you include your questions as direct speech, in some other way, or not at all? Or will you use a mixture of these approaches?	
How formal do you want your language to be? Will you make your own descriptive comment more formal than your interviewee's words?	
What kind of tone do you want your article to have? Would a light humorous touch be appropriate, or a more serious and respectful tone?	
How can you give the interview an effective ending? Will you refer back to the opening, make a joke or use some other technique?	

English Frameworking 3: Teacher's Resources © HarperCollinsPublishers 2002

Analyse, review, comment: Journalism

Worksheet 80

Name:
Form:

Have sharks always inspired terror?

The first paragraph from a magazine article on sharks is set under the heading 'Have sharks always inspired terror?' This paragraph has been reduced to bullet form notes (below). Your task is:

In groups – Decide on a logical order in which to put the information.

On your own – Rewrite the bullets as an effective and cohesive paragraph of continuous prose in Standard English. You can add or rearrange words but you cannot introduce new facts or ideas. Remember that the paragraph should answer the question 'Have sharks always inspired terror?'

- Turn of 19th/20th century – general belief sharks were harmless.
- 1916 – Great White shark killed 4 off New Jersey, removing both legs from one victim.
- 1891 – US millionaire Hermann Oelrichs offered $500 to anyone who proved a shark had attacked anyone.
- 5th century BC – sharks described as man-eating animals by Greek historian Herodotus.
- 1916 – first recorded outbreak of hysteria about sharks – used by Peter Benchley in novel *Jaws*.
- 1915 – New York Times editorial ('Let us do justice to sharks') says sharks are timid and couldn't bite through a man's leg.

Now get back in groups and compare the results. Choose the most effective paragraph, which presents the information in the clearest, liveliest and most coherent way.

Feed back to the class. Which paragraph explains the precise connection between the ideas most clearly and entertainingly?

English Frameworking 3: Teacher's Resources   © HarperCollinsPublishers 2002

Analyse, review, comment: Journalism

Worksheet 81

Analysing the structure of an article on fox hunting

Name:
Form:

In pairs, read the article 'Should there be a ban on hunting' on page 103 and decide whether each paragraph is intended:

1 To provide news and explanation about the vote in Parliament on hunting, or

2 To provide analysis of the underlying issues of the rights and wrongs of fox hunting, backed up by the opinions of the interested parties.

Put a tick in the relevant box in the grid below. Put a tick in both boxes if you think the paragraph intends to do both things, and leave both boxes blank if you think the paragraph has another purpose.

	1 News and explanation about the vote	2 Underlying issues and opinions
Para 1 'A vote by MPs …'	☐	☐
Para 2 'Surveys suggest …'	☐	☐
Para 3 'MPs will have …'	☐	☐
Para 4 'Even if the vote …'	☐	☐
Para 5 'The present hunting bill …'	☐	☐
Para 6 'Supporters of hunting …'	☐	☐
Para 7 'The Burns Report …'	☐	☐
Para 8 'Then there are …'	☐	☐
Para 9 'If the issue …'	☐	☐
Display box 'What they said …'	☐	☐

Feed back to the class. Why do you think the writer has structured the article in this way? Is it effective?

Analyse, review, comment: Journalism

Worksheet 82

Brainstorming slang

pg 104

Name:
Form:

As you discuss what you know about slang, jot your ideas down in the grid below.

What is the definition of slang?

What words or phrases are classified as 'slang'?

What are the functions and characteristics of non-Standard English?

When is it appropriate to use slang?

English Frameworking 3: Teacher's Resources © HarperCollins*Publishers* 2002

Analyse, review, comment: Journalism — Worksheet 83

Slang: evidence and opinions

> **slang** *n.* 1 language of a highly colloquial type, considered as below the level of educated standard speech, and consisting either of new words or of current words employed in some special sense. 2 language of a low or vulgar type. 3 the special vocabulary or phraseology of a particular calling or profession (*racing slang; schoolboy slang*)

The panel

The question:
The new Penguin English Dictionary contains a lexicon of teenage slang. Will this damage their use of 'proper' English?

John Wells
Professor of phonetics, University College London
All social groups like to distinguish themselves by having their own words and jargon. This is not dangerous or unhealthy. Every group of young people develops its own words. These are additions to the language, extras that don't replace it. People who don't understand what's going on see it as a threat. When I was a child, there were words defined as American but now they are part of everyday language. And in Victorian times, people were shocked by words like 'scientist' because they were used to using the words 'man of science'.

Nick Bell
Managing director of teenfront.com, Age 17
I don't think slang is a bad thing. We should expect language to develop over time. The use of emailing and text messaging means that teenagers are communicating much more in a written form. The language used is more relaxed, more short, snappy and to the point – as society changes the language follows. I think language is more slangy because society is being dictated far more by the youth. There's a lot of US phrases and sayings used by TV characters like Ali G. But while teenagers use a lot of slang, we're still capable of using traditional English.

Nigel Wilcockson
Publishing director, Penguin books
I don't think the use of slang among teenagers is either healthy or unhealthy so much as inevitable. And it always has been. Effectively, slang is playing with language. For the past 200 years every single generation has said that the upcoming generation doesn't speak the way they do, but the language hasn't fallen apart as a result. I think that what is happening now is that fashions come and go more quickly. You see so many words coming in directly from the pop scene or from Hollywood.

Chris Ainoo
An editor at the Children's Express magazine
I think slang is a bad thing. If you are always talking in slang then the language you need when you want to talk or write something properly isn't always there and you have to dig very deep to find the words. For a while, everyone was saying 'Yeah baby' and a couple of years ago people were referring to each other as 'brer' (short for brother) but that isn't really around now. If I'm writing an article for Children's Express I will use a lot more 'proper' English than when I'm talking, although I will still use some slang. Slang is bad, but I like it.

Tony Thorne
Director, language centre, King's College London
There's no way slang actually damages young people's ability to use standard English because young people are particularly expert and adept at code switching – knowing how to use the right language for the right circumstances. Children don't use slang all the time, they use it for special effect in intimate situations or when they want to emphasise membership of a group. Slang dramatises and brightens up their speech. Slang works in exactly the same way as poetry, making use of metaphor, irony and alliteration. Young people are not so dumb as to use slang in job interviews or essays.

Gila Goldberg
Teacher of English as a foreign language
Slang will always be part of language, and language is a changing, dynamic thing – we don't speak as Shakespeare spoke. Slang is a way of belonging, but when I teach people English I don't teach them slang because I think it makes them lazy. They actually have to do less to communicate when they use slang and they lose their ability to articulate things properly. Slang has a place in language, but children and teenagers need to realise that you can't use it to write official letters and that it doesn't belong everywhere. We should make sure we teach people proper English.

Poetry analysis notice board

Writer's purpose:

Theme:

Narrative perspective: autobiographical; autobiographical style – persona; monologue; third person etc

Tone: formal, informal, serious, sad, comic, mocking, ironic, etc.

Form: overall structure; line structure; rhythm; rhyme

Style:

- choice of vocabulary – (simple, elaborate, varied)
- word order (diction)
- imagery and figurative language (including simile, metaphor, personification)
- sound effects (repetition, alliteration, assonance, onomatopoeia)

Plan, draft, present: 20th-century poetry

Worksheet 85

Constructing a sonnet

Not only marble but the plastic toys from cornflake packets will outlive this

rhyme: I can't immortalise you, love – our joys will lie unnoticed in the vault

of time. When Mrs Thatcher has been cast in bronze and her administration

is a page in some O-level text-book, when the dons have analysed the story

of our age, when travel firms sell tours of outer space and aeroplanes take

off without a sound and Tulse Hill has become a trendy place and Upper

Norwood's on the underground your beauty and my name will be forgotten –

my love is true but all my verse is rotten.

> Not only marble but the plastic toys
> From cornflake packets will outlive this rhyme:
> I can't immortalise you, love – our joys
> Will lie unnoticed in the vault of time.
> When Mrs Thatcher has been cast in bronze
> And her administration is a page
> In some O-level text-book, when the dons
> Have analysed the story of our age,
> When travel firms sell tours of outer space
> And aeroplanes take off without a sound
> And Tulse Hill has become a trendy place
> And Upper Norwood's on the underground
>   Your beauty and my name will be forgotten –
>   My love is true but all my verse is rotten.

Plan, draft, present: 20th-century poetry

Worksheet 86

Evaluating your speaking and listening (1)

pg 112

Name:
Form:

Fill in the grid below, highlighting the points that are particularly relevant to you, and decide on your speaking and listening targets for this section. Write your targets on the back of the worksheet.

Feature under consideration	Yes/No/ Sometimes	Comment/ way forward
Discussion – speaking and listening		
Approach		
Do I value discussion time?		
Do I contribute sufficiently?		
Do I try to avoid speaking?		
Do I let others speak?		
Do I tend to shout and try to force others to agree with me?		
Do I tend to try to dominate discussion too much?		
Do I have a tendency to want to score points off people?		
Do I find other people's contributions interesting?		
Do I listen to what others say even when I don't agree?		
Do I show sensitivity to other people's ideas?		
Do I adjust my views in the light of other people's?		
Do I encourage others to speak?		
Do I ask questions and encourage ideas to be thought through?		
Am I willing to maintain a minority viewpoint?		
Skills		
Do I express my points clearly and fluently?		
Do I support my points with appropriate evidence?		
Do I link my points coherently?		
Do I use formal language appropriately?		
Do I listen to ideas and contribute appropriately?		
Do I build on other people's contributions by constructive comments or questions?		
Can I change the way I talk to suit a range of situations?		
Can I contribute confidently in formal situations?		
Formal presentations – speaking		
Do I make eye contact with the audience?		
Do I speak with expression?		
Do I express my points clearly and fluently?		
Do I feel confident when making a formal presentation?		
Do I use formal language appropriately?		
Do I use the appropriate technical vocabulary?		
Can I speak without notes or from brief prompt points?		
Can I keep an audience's attention?		

English Frameworking 3: Teacher's Resources © HarperCollins Publishers 2002

Plan, draft, present: 20th-century poetry

Worksheet 87a

Speaking and listening record (1)

pg 113

Name:
Form:

Lesson and activity – tick all activities in which you took an active part	Comment on your participation and progress towards achieving targets
1 Lesson: Poems don't have to rhyme	
• Listening to sound of 'This Is Just to Say'	
• Partnership discussion on effect of 'This Is Just to Say'	
• Class discussion on 'This Is Just to Say'	
• Listening to 'The Red Wheelbarrow'	
• Class discussion on 'The Red Wheelbarrow'	
• Participation in group discussion to select poems	
• Presentation of poems	
2 Lesson: Playing with syntax	
• Discussion of 'According to My Mood'	
• Listening to 'anyone lived in a pretty how town'	
• Initial discussion of 'anyone lived in a pretty how town'	
• Group analysis of verse	
• Class discussion of 'anyone lived in a pretty how town'	
• Plenary discussion	
3 Lesson: Inspired by art	
• Brainstorm on art as source of inspiration	
• Listening to 'Musée des Beaux Arts' and feedback	
• Partnership discussion on 'Musée des Beaux Arts' and feedback	
• Listening to 'Not My Best Side' and 'I Would Like to Be a Dot in a Painting by Miró'	
• Group discussion on 'Not My Best Side' and 'I Would Like to Be a Dot in a Painting by Miró' and feedback	
• Plenary discussion	

English Frameworking 3: Teacher's Resources © HarperCollinsPublishers 2002

Plan, draft, present: 20th-century poetry — Worksheet 87b

Speaking and listening record (2)

Name:
Form:

pg 113

Lesson and activity – tick all activities in which you took an active part	Comment on your participation and progress towards achieving targets
4 Lesson: Expressing grief	
• Brainstorm on love/grief as source of poetry	
• Listening to 'Funeral Blues' and 'Long Distance'	
• Partnership discussion on 'Funeral Blues' and feedback	
• Group discussion on 'Long Distance' and feedback	
• Plenary discussion	
5 Lesson: Preparing to write an essay	
• Sorting activity on how to prepare	
• Class discussion of 'Death of a Naturalist'	
• Group discussion of 'In Mrs Tilscher's Class' and feedback	
• Plenary discussion	
6 Lesson: Comparing two poems	
• Class discussion of essay question	
• Group sorting activity	
• Explaining key points of your essay to partner	
• Plenary discussion	
7 Lesson: Organizing group presentations	
• Problem-solving activity	
• Groupwork preparing presentation	
• Plenary discussion	
8 Lesson: Presenting a favourite poem	
• Refining your presentation	
• Participation in presentation	
• Plenary discussion	

English Frameworking 3: Teacher's Resources   © HarperCollinsPublishers 2002

anyone lived in a pretty how town

anyone lived in a pretty how town
(with up so floating many bells down)
spring summer autumn winter
he sang his didn't he danced his did.

Women and men (both little and small)
cared for anyone not at all
they sowed their isn't they reaped
   their same
sun moon stars rain

children guessed (but only a few
and down they forgot as up they grew
autumn winter spring summer)
that noone loved him more by more

when by now and tree by leaf
she laughed his joy she cried his grief
bird by snow and stir by still
anyone's any was all to her

someones married their everyones
laughed their cryings and did their
   dance
(sleep wake hope and then) they
said their nevers they slept their dream

stars rain sun moon
(and only the snow can begin to explain
how children are apt to forget
   to remember
with up so floating many bells down)

one day anyone died i guess
(and noone stooped to kiss his face)
busy folk buried them side by side
little by little and was by was

all by all and deep by deep
and more by more they dream their
   sleep
noone and anyone earth by april
wish by spirit and if by yes.

Women and men (both dong and ding)
summer autumn winter spring
reaped their sowing and went
   their came
sun moon stars rain

E. E. Cummings (1894–1962) went to France to drive an ambulance in the First World War after his graduation from Havard University. Through a misunderstanding, he spent a considerable time in a French prison, and wrote a novel about this experience. Cummings was a prolific poet who experimented with typographical innovations.

Use of language in 'anyone lived in a pretty how town'

Plan, draft, present: 20th-century poetry — Worksheet 89

Group 1
Women and men (both little and small)
cared for anyone not at all
they sowed their isn't they reaped their same
sun moon stars rain

Group 2
children guessed (but only a few
and down they forgot as up they grew
autumn winter spring summer)
that noone loved him more by more

Group 3
when by now and tree by leaf
she laughed his joy she cried his grief
bird by snow and stir by still
anyone's any was all to her

Group 4
someones married their everyones
laughed their cryings and did their dance
(sleep wake hope and then) they
said their nevers they slept their dream

Group 5
stars rain sun moon
(and only the snow can begin to explain
how children are apt to forget to remember
with up so floating many bells down)

Group 6
one day anyone died i guess
(and noone stooped to kiss his face)
busy folk buried them side by side
little by little and was by was

Group 7
all by all and deep by deep
and more by more they dream their sleep
noone and anyone earth by april
wish by spirit and if by yes.

Group 8
Women and men (both dong and ding)
summer autumn winter spring
reaped their sowing and went their came
sun moon stars rain

Musée des Beaux Arts

Musée des Beaux Arts[1]

About suffering they were never wrong,
The Old Masters:[2] how well they understood
Its human position; how it takes place
While someone else is eating or opening a window or just walking dully along;
How, when the aged are reverently, passionately waiting
For the miraculous birth,[3] there always must be
Children who did not specially want it to happen, skating
On a pond at the edge of a wood:
They never forgot
That even the dreadful martyrdom[4] must run its course
Anyhow in a corner, some untidy spot
Where the dogs go on with their doggy life and the torturer's horse
Scratches its innocent behind on a tree.

In Brueghel's *Icarus*,[5] for instance: how everything turns away
Quite leisurely from the disaster; the ploughman may
Have heard the splash, the forsaken cry,
But for him it was not an important failure; the sun shone
As it had to on the white legs disappearing into the green
Water; and the expensive delicate ship that must have seen
Something amazing, a boy falling out of the sky,
Had somewhere to get to and sailed calmly on.

W. H. Auden

---

[1] museum of fine art, art gallery
[2] the great European painters of the period 1500 to 1800
[3] the birth of Christ, the subject of many Old Master paintings
[4] the Massacre of the Innocents, the slaughter of the children of Bethlehem by King Herod, another subject painted by Brueghel and others
[5] a character from Greek myth who escaped captivity by flying with wings made from wax and feathers. He ignored his father's warning not to fly too near the sun: the wax melted and he fell into the Aegean Sea and drowned.

W. H. Auden (1907–1973) was born in York but lived for much of his life in America. He studied natural sciences, then English, at Oxford University. By the age of twenty-three he had become recognized as the leader of a new generation of English poets. Much of his poetry focuses on the central issues of the 20th century.

Not My Best Side

I

Not my best side, I'm afraid.
The artist didn't give me a chance to
Pose properly, and as you can see,
Poor chap, he had this obsession with
Triangles, so he left off two of my
Feet. I didn't comment at the time
(What, after all, are two feet
To a monster?) but afterwards
I was sorry for the bad publicity.
Why, I said to myself, should my conqueror
Be so ostentatiously[1] beardless, and ride
A horse with a deformed neck and square hoofs?
Why should my victim be so
Unattractive as to be inedible,
And why should she have me literally
On a string? I don't mind dying
Ritually, since I always rise again,
But I should have liked a little more blood
To show that they were taking me seriously.

II

It's hard for a girl to be sure if
She wants to be rescued. I mean, I quite
Took to the dragon. It's nice to be
Liked, if you know what I mean. He was
So nicely physical, with his claws
And lovely green skin, and that sexy tail,
And the way he looked at me,
He made me feel he was all ready to
Eat me. And any girl enjoys that.
So when this boy turned up wearing machinery,
On a really *dangerous* horse, to be honest
I didn't much fancy him. I mean,
What was he like underneath the hardware?
He might have acne, blackheads or even
Bad breath for all I could tell, but the dragon –
Well, you could see all his equipment
At a glance. Still, what could I do?
The dragon got himself beaten by the boy,
And a girl's got to think of her future.

III

I have diplomas in Dragon
Management and Virgin Reclamation.
My horse is the latest model, with
Automatic transmission[2] and built-in
Obsolescence.[3] My spear is custom-built,
And my prototype armour
Still on the secret list.
You can't do better than me at the moment.
I'm qualified and equipped to the
Eyebrow. So why be difficult?
Don't you want to be killed and/or rescued
In the most contemporary way? Don't
You want to carry out the roles
That sociology and myth have designed for you?
Don't you realise that, by being choosy,
You are endangering job prospects
In the spear- and horse-building industries?
What in any case does it matter what
You want. You're in my way.

U. A. Fanthorpe

---

[1] *showily*
[2] *system of gears etc. that transmit power from the engine to the driving wheels of a vehicle*
[3] *state of being out of date*

U. A. Fanthorpe was born in Kent in 1929. She was head of English at an independent girls' school until 1970, and in 1974 became clerk/receptionist in a Bristol Hospital. When she was nearly 50 her first collection of poems, *Side Effects*, which includes 'Not My Best Side', was published.

I Would Like to Be a Dot in a Painting by Miró

I would like to be a dot in a painting by Miró.

Barely distinguishable from other dots,
It's true, but quite uniquely placed.
And from my dark centre

I'd survey the beauty of the linescape
And wonder – would it be worthwhile
To roll myself towards the lemon stripe,

Centrally poised, and push my curves
Against its edge, to get myself
A little extra attention?

But it's fine where I am.
I'll never make out what's going on
Around me, and that's the joy of it.

The fact that I'm not a perfect circle
Makes me more interesting in this world.
People will stare forever –

Even the most unemotional get excited.
So here I am, on the edge of animation,
A dream, a dance, a fantastic construction,

A child's adventure.
And nothing in this tawny sky
Can get too close, or move too far away.

Moniza Alvi

Moniza Alvi was born in Pakistan in 1954 and moved to England when she was a child. Much of her poetry includes fantasy.

Plan, draft, present: Formal essays and presentations — Worksheet 93

Preparing to write an essay

Analyse the question	**Highlight on the grid points of significant comparison and difference**
Read both poems several times to understand them in their own right before attempting to compare them	**Plan essay using analysis grid to help you (remember Point, Evidence, Comment)**
Re-read the question carefully	**Plan interesting, relevant introduction**
Use analysis grid to help analyse both writers' purpose, theme, narrative perspective, form and style with brief evidence	**Start writing essay**

Plan, draft, present: Formal essays and presentations — Worksheet 94

Analysing 'Death of a Naturalist'

Name:
Form:

Fill in the analysis grid below on Seamus Heaney's poem 'Death of a Naturalist'.

Aspect	Point	Evidence
Writer's purpose		
Theme		
Narrative perspective		
Tone		
Form		
Consider: • overall structure (look at layout on page 121 of Student's Book)		
• line structure		
• rhyme		
• rhythm		
Style – language		
Consider: • choice of vocabulary (simple, elaborate, varied)		
• word order (diction)		
• imagery and figurative language (simile, metaphor, personification)		
• sound effects (repetition, alliteration, assonance, onomatopoeia)		
Quality of ending		

Plan, draft, present: Formal essays and presentations — Worksheet 95

In Mrs Tilscher's Class

Name:
Form:

IN MRS TILSCHER'S CLASS

You could travel up the Blue Nile
with your finger, tracing the route
while Mrs Tilscher chanted the scenery.
Tana. Ethiopia. Khartoum. Aswân.
That for an hour, then a skittle of milk
and the chalky Pyramids rubbed into dust.
A window opened with a long pole.
The laugh of a bell swung by a running child.

This was better than home. Enthralling books.
The classroom glowed like a sweetshop.
Sugar paper. Coloured shapes. Brady and Hindley[1]
faded, like the faint, uneasy smudge of a mistake.
Mrs Tilscher loved you. Some mornings, you found
she'd left a gold star by your name.
The scent of a pencil slowly, carefully, shaved.
A xylophone's nonsense heard from another form.

Over the Easter term the inky tadpoles changed
from commas into exclamation marks. Three frogs
hopped in the playground, freed by a dunce,
followed by a line of kids, jumping and croaking
away from the lunch queue. A rough boy
told you how you were born. You kicked him, but stared
at your parents, appalled, when you got back home.

That feverish July, the air tasted of electricity.
A tangible alarm made you always untidy, hot,
fractious under the heavy, sexy sky. You asked her
how you were born and Mrs Tilscher smiled,
then turned away. Reports were handed out.
You ran through the gates, impatient to be grown,
as the sky split open into a thunderstorm.

Carol Ann Duffy

[1] *notorious child-murderers in the 1960s*

Carol Ann Duffy was born in Glasgow of Irish parents in 1955 and grew up in Stafford. Among the most popular of modern poets, she is particularly known for her dramatic monologues.

Plan, draft, present: Formal essays and presentations — **Worksheet 96**

Analysing 'In Mrs Tilscher's Class'

Name:
Form:

Fill in the analysis grid below on Carol Ann Duffy's poem 'In Mrs Tilscher's Class'.

Aspect	Point	Evidence
Writer's purpose		
Theme		
Narrative perspective		
Tone		
Form		
Consider: • overall structure (look at layout on Worksheet 95)		
• line structure		
• rhyme		
• rhythm		
Style – language		
Consider: • choice of vocabulary (simple, elaborate, varied)		
• word order (diction)		
• imagery and figurative language (simile, metaphor, personification)		
• sound effects (repetition, alliteration, assonance, onomatopoeia)		
Quality of ending		

Plan, draft, present: Formal essays and presentations — Worksheet 97

Selecting the correct register
(pg 122)

Sentence starters that are NOT appropriate for this formal essay	Sentence starters that are appropriate for this formal essay
Both poems were a good laugh especially the line about frogs farting and …	It is possible that the poet chose to split this line across the only verse break in the poem because …
The best bit in Carol's poem was …	The line that I liked best in Carol Ann Duffy's poem is …
And another thing I liked was …	Both poets have chosen to focus on …
When I was at primary school we had frogspawn too and one day I …	'But best of all' tells the reader that the child just loved the …
There was lots and lots of onomatopoeia in 'Death of a Naturalist' …	The poet has chosen words like 'slap' and 'plop' so the reader not only …
I'm going to start off by telling you what the poems are about and then I'm going to …	Frogspawn must make a strong impression on school children because both poets …
In my group everyone thought that …	Frogspawn has been chosen by both poets because …
In English we have been reading two poems about childhood memories …	The line 'but stared at your parents, appalled' helps the reader picture the child's sense of …

English Frameworking 3: Teacher's Resources © HarperCollins Publishers 2002

Plan, draft, present: Formal essays and presentations | Worksheet 98

Reviewing your writing (pg 123)

Name
Form

Look at your most recent writing targets and decide if you have achieved them.
Use the grid below to help you analyse what writing skills still need developing.

Writing activities in this section	Successful aspects	Skills that need developing
Creative writing. I wrote poems within differing poetic forms. I can:		
• choose appropriate form		
• choose good vocabulary		
• use imagery and sound effects well.		
Presentation. I selected the best of my own poems and decided how to present it to maximize its effect. I have:		
• design and presentational skills		
• legible handwriting		
• IT layout skills.		
Evaluation & recording. I evaluated speaking and listening skills and kept a written record of my input into speaking and listening activities. I can:		
• select key points and sum them up		
• reflect.		
Note taking & planning. I used a grid to analyse poems and to help plan a formal essay. I can:		
• think coherently		
• select key points and see links		
• sum up points.		
Formal essay. I wrote a formal timed essay. I can:		
• shape ideas rapidly		
• link ideas in cohesive paragraphs		
• support points with evidence		
• integrate quotations		
• sustain formal English		
• write legibly at speed		
• maintain technical accuracy (spelling, syntax, punctuation).		

List your revised writing targets here:

•
•
•

156

English Frameworking 3: Teacher's Resources © HarperCollinsPublishers 2002

Plan, draft, present: Formal essays and presentations

Worksheet 99

Which poem did you prefer?

pg 124

Name:
Form:

Fill in the grid below. Your first choice should be rated 1; second choice 2, etc. If a number of poems tie for the same place you should take this into account in your rating. For example, if you give three poems the rating 2, the next poem should be rated as 5.

Name of poem and poet	Rating	Brief explanation of rating
'Rising Five' by Norman Nicholson (page 109)		
Sonnet 138 by William Shakespeare (page 110)		
Sonnet by Wendy Cope (page 111)		
'This Is Just to Say' by William Carlos Williams (page 113)		
'The Red Wheelbarrow' by William Carlos Williams (page 113)		
'According to My Mood' by Benjamin Zephaniah (page 114)		
'anyone lived in a pretty how town' by E. E. Cummings (Worksheet 88)		
'Musée des Beaux Arts' by W. H. Auden (Worksheet 90)		
'Not My Best Side' by U. A. Fanthorpe (Worksheet 91)		
'I Would Like to be a Dot in a Painting by Miró' by Moniza Alvi (Worksheet 92)		
'Funeral Blues' by W. H. Auden (page 118)		
From 'Long Distance' by Tony Harrison (page 119)		
'Death of a Naturalist' by Seamus Heaney (page 121)		
'In Mrs Tilscher's Class' by Carol Ann Duffy (Worksheet 95)		

Plan, draft, present: Formal essays and presentations

Worksheet **100**

Evaluation grid for group poetry presentations
pg 126

Name:
Form:

Group number and poem focused on	Main strengths of presentation	Key aspects that need improving

Evaluating your speaking and listening (2)

Plan, draft, present: Formal essays and presentations — Worksheet 101

Name:
Form:

Fill in the grid below, highlighting the points that are particularly relevant to you, and decide on your speaking and listening targets for this section.

Feature under consideration	Yes/No/ Sometimes	Comment/ Way forward
Discussion – speaking and listening		
Approach		
Do I value discussion time?		
Do I contribute sufficiently?		
Do I try to avoid speaking?		
Do I let others speak?		
Do I tend to shout and try to force others to agree with me?		
Do I tend to try to dominate discussion too much?		
Do I have a tendency to want to score points off people?		
Do I find other people's contributions interesting?		
Do I listen to what others say even when I don't agree?		
Do I show sensitivity to other people's ideas?		
Do I adjust my views in the light of other people's?		
Do I encourage others to speak?		
Do I ask questions and encourage ideas to be thought through?		
Am I willing to maintain a minority viewpoint?		
Skills		
Do I express my points clearly and fluently?		
Do I support my points with appropriate evidence?		
Do I link my points coherently?		
Do I use formal language appropriately?		
Do I listen to ideas and contribute appropriately?		
Do I build on other people's contributions by constructive comments or questions?		
Can I change the way I talk to suit a range of situations?		
Can I contribute confidently in formal situations?		
Formal presentations – speaking		
Do I make eye contact with the audience?		
Do I speak with expression?		
Do I express my points clearly and fluently?		
Do I feel confident when making a formal presentation?		
Do I use formal language appropriately?		
Do I use the appropriate technical vocabulary?		
Can I speak without notes or from brief prompt points?		
Can I keep an audience's attention?		

English Frameworking 3: Teacher's Resources © HarperCollins Publishers 2002

Preparing for NCTs

Worksheet 102

The National Curriculum Test in English

Name:
Form:

This worksheet gives you an idea of what the English NCT consists of. (Note that examinations change from time to time, so the format set out below may vary slightly.)

Paper 1 (Levels 4–7)

This paper tests your **reading and writing**.

You will be given **15 minutes'** reading time. During this time you can read the paper and make notes, but you may not begin to write your answers.

You then have **1 hour and 30 minutes** to complete the paper.

There are three sections:

Section A – Reading. Often a non-fiction/media text from a newspaper or magazine is set, approximately two sides of A4 in length. There will be **two questions** on the extract which usually ask you to focus on the language and style of the writing in different parts of the text. You are advised to spend about **30 minutes** on this section. (These two questions together will be worth about 17 marks.)

Section B – Reading. The second text in the paper may be fiction or non-fiction, and is usually shorter, about one side of A4. There will be **one question** which is likely to ask you to analyse the effects created by the author and explain how they have been successful. You are advised to spend **20 minutes** on this section. (This question is worth about 11 marks.)

Section C – Writing. This is the only part of the paper where you are given a choice. There are usually three options, generally linked with the content of the reading extracts in some way. Each option will ask you to write in a different form and purpose. Sometimes the audience is stated, but whether it is or not, it is something that you need to consider. You will **choose one of the options** only and spend **35 minutes** on this section, which includes planning, as well as writing. (This question is worth about 33 marks.)

This should leave you with **5 minutes** at the end to check through your work.

Paper 2 (Levels 4–7)

This paper tests your knowledge and understanding of the **Shakespeare play** that you have been studying.

The test is **1 hour and 15 minutes** long.

You will be given a **booklet containing the set scenes** for each play – no notes or glossaries, just the plain text.

There will be two questions on each of the three plays that have been set for study. You need to look for the questions on your play only, e.g. *Macbeth*. **Answer only one question**.

Leave at least **5 minutes** to check through your work carefully at the end.

Extension Paper (Level 8 and EP*)

For some students who could achieve level 8, there is also an extension paper. A few students take this paper, but it is more difficult. Your teacher will discuss whether it is appropriate for you to take this extra paper.

It is **1 hour 30 minutes** long.

It tests **reading and writing** in a similar way to paper 1, but the extracts and tasks that are set are more complex and exacting. In order to be successful, you need to have a high level of understanding and vocabulary, as well as the ability to express your ideas clearly and with interest.

In addition to the test papers, your teacher will also give you a **teacher assessment** for the standard you have achieved in your English classwork and homework during the year. This assessment includes one for **speaking and listening**, which is not assessed in the test.

*exceptional performance

Preparing for NCTs — Worksheet **103**

Reading skills and levels

Name:
Form:

The statements in the boxes below describe the reading skills that students should show at each of the NC levels 4 to 8, but they haven't been given in the right order.

1. Discuss which statements belong to which NC level, and write the level number (4, 5, 6, 7 or 8) in the box.

2. When you have agreed on the right order, highlight the key words in each statement that have helped you to decide the range of difficulty and the progression as you move from one level to another.

Response to non-fiction and media texts

	Statement – Students can:	Level
G	identify layers of meaning and comment on their significance and effect	
H	respond to a range of texts and begin to use inference and deduction	
I	show appreciation of a range of texts, select and analyse information and ideas, and comment on how these are conveyed in different texts	
J	select essential points, using inference and deduction where appropriate	
K	show understanding of the ways in which meaning and information are conveyed in a range of texts	

Response to literature

	Statement – Students can:	Level
L	articulate personal and critical responses to literature showing awareness of their thematic, structural and linguistic features	
M	evaluate how authors achieve their effects through the use of linguistic, structural and presentational devices	
N	give personal responses to literary texts, referring to aspects of language, structure and themes in justifying their views	
O	identify key features, themes and characters and select sentences, phrases and relevant information to support their views	
P	understand significant ideas, themes, events and characters	

English Frameworking 3: Teacher's Resources © HarperCollins*Publishers* 2002

Preparing for NCTs

Worksheet 104

The shorter reading question

Name:
Form:

Section A

Read the following passage. Then answer the question below.

The passage is an account by the actress and writer Fanny Kemble of a journey made on the Manchester to Liverpool railway in 1830, using Stephenson's Rocket, which had just won the prize for being the most efficient locomotive of its day. She was just twenty-one at the time and was probably the first woman ever to travel by train.

1 My father knew several of the gentlemen most deeply interested in the undertaking [the Liverpool-Manchester railway], and Stephenson having proposed a trial trip as far as the fifteen-mile
5 viaduct,[1] they, with infinite kindness, invited him and permitted me to accompany them; allowing me, moreover, the place which I felt to be one of supreme honour, by the side of Stephenson. He was a rather stern-featured man, with a dark and deeply-
10 marked countenance;[2] his speech was strongly inflected with his native Northumbrian accent.

   We were introduced to the little engine which was to drag us along the rails. This snorting little animal, which I felt rather inclined to pat, was then
15 harnessed to our carriage, and, Mr. Stephenson having taken me on the bench of the engine with him, we started at about ten miles an hour. The steam-horse being ill-adapted for going up and down hill, the road was kept at a certain level, and
20 appeared sometimes to sink below the surface of the earth, and sometimes to rise above it. Almost at starting it was cut through the solid rock, which formed a wall on either side of it, about sixty feet high. You can't imagine how strange it seemed to be
25 journeying on thus, without any visible cause of progress other than the magical machine, with its flying white breath and rhythmical, unvarying pace. We were to go only fifteen miles, that distance being sufficient to show the speed of the engine.
30 After proceeding through this rocky defile,[3] we presently found ourselves raised upon embankments ten or twelve feet high; we then came to a moss, or swamp, of considerable extent, on which no human foot could tread without sinking, and yet it bore the
35 road which bore us. This had been the great stumbling-block in the minds of the committee of the House of Commons; but Mr. Stephenson has succeeded in overcoming it.

   We had now come fifteen miles, and stopped
40 where the road traversed[4] a wide and deep valley. Stephenson made me alight and led me down to the bottom of this ravine, over which, in order to keep his road level, he has thrown a magnificent viaduct of nine arches, the middle one of which is seventy
45 feet high, through which we saw the whole of this beautiful little valley. We then rejoined the rest of the party, and the engine having received its supply of water, the carriage was placed behind it, for it cannot turn, and was set off at its utmost speed,
50 thirty-five miles an hour, swifter than a bird flies (for they tried the experiment with a snipe). You cannot conceive what the sensation of cutting the air was; the motion is as smooth as possible, too. I could have either read or written.

Fanny Kemble *from* 'Record of a Girlhood', 1878

[1] *a long bridge*
[2] *face*
[3] *a long, narrow pass*
[4] *crossed*

Explain how the writer has described her experience of the journey to an audience who had never travelled by train themselves.

In your answer you should comment on:

- the way in which the writer introduces this new experience of a journey by train to an audience who would not have experienced anything like it themselves;
- how the writer's use of descriptive language and imagery makes the passage interesting to the reader;
- how the thoughts and feelings concerning the writer's personal experience contribute to the effect she creates.

Refer to words and phrases in the passage to support your ideas.

11 marks

Preparing for NCTs

Worksheet 105a

The longer reading question (1)

Name
Form

Flat-track Family

Winding through the Peak District, old railways have been made into cycle paths. Perfect for a spin with the kids, says Dan Joyce

'You said this bit would be flat!' My nine-year-old son is unimpressed with my map reading. That morning we'd pushed the bikes up a mile-long 1-in-8 road to get to the
5 High Peak Trail. 'It used to be a railway,' I'd told him, 'and trains don't go uphill.' But the trucks on what was the Cromford and High Peak Railway had done exactly that. At the top of our unexpected hill we found the house-sized **static** steam engine that used to haul them up.

Of course, you expect hills in the Peak District. Unfold any map of the area and the
10 **contour** lines cluster together like the **whorls** on a fingerprint. Scattered around on the roads are those tell-tale 'V' signs: one 'V' for 1 in 7 (Very hard), two for 1 in 5 (Very, Very hard). And as all the old-stone towns are in the valleys, sooner or later you'll hit a hard climb if you travel between. Racing cyclists relish these roads, but if you're cycling with children and luggage, as we were, you'll walk. On quiet roads it's more leisurely
15 than it sounds; we took the time to chat, eat sweets, admire the views, watch the kestrel hovering. It's only the Peak District's heavily trafficked roads – the As and Bs – that are unpleasant.

Yet you can escape both traffic and hills, courtesy of old converted train lines that haven't seen track or trains for decades. The 17-mile High Peak Trail is just one of them,
20 and other than the steep climb at the end – it was built as a transport link to cross the high ground between two canals either side of the Pennines – its cuttings and **embankments** keep it flat. It joins the Tissington Trail, a 13-mile path on the site of the old Ashbourne–Buxton railway line, which is less exposed and flatter still. Only a few miles further on is the best and easiest of the lot: the Manifold Way, a pan-flat eight-mile
25 path along the bottom of a stunning limestone valley, once the home of the Leek and Manifold Light Railway. Foot and mouth disease shut the trails, but they're open again now, offering cyclists and walkers a network of nearly 40 off-road miles through some of Britain's best scenery. Yet the **gradients** are so easy that a five-year-old could ride most of it; we saw many children doing just that, some still with stabilisers.

30 Bike-hire centres with **adjacent** car parks sit on all the trails, so you don't have to pedal (or push) your own bikes to get there. If you don't think your children can manage the mileage - and going west on the 1,000ft High Peak Trail into the teeth of the **prevailing** wind, it can be hard – you can hire a variety of child-carrying conveyances. There are childseats for toddlers, two-seater trailers for teenies or **siblings**, and
35 trailerbikes for bigger kids.

We met cyclists every mile or two, and just once a stream of huffing **orienteers**. Otherwise we had the lush, rolling landscape of the Derbyshire Dales to ourselves. The trail twisted and turned to keep its height, through **lichen-crusted** rock cuttings and over old stone embankments that looked like Hadrian's Wall. Lambs filled the high fields
40 while finches flitted between hedges.

Preparing for NCTs Worksheet **105b**

The longer reading question (2)

Name
Form

The High Peak Trail cuts across open countryside with no halts en route. Once you leave Middleton Top, you have a dozen miles or so to get to Hartington or Parsley Hay. In contrast, the Tissington Trail links villages, and the Manifold Way has a couple of tea shops along the way, making both of them easier for families to complete.

45 We, never had any problems – other than a two-mile hill on a busy road we shouldn't have been on, coming out of Chesterfield – but whenever you're riding with children you need to look to their needs. Take plenty of sugary snacks. Not only will they keep morale high, they'll providing instant energy to keep little legs turning. Unless it's genuinely hot, children will often need one layer of clothes more than you 50 because they won't generate as much heat (they won't be working as hard!).

Keen fathers need to remember that they're not in the Tour de Wherever, either. The cycling is a means to an end. Enjoy the landscape and the nearby attractions - there's everything from theme parks to standing stones in the Peak District, all close together.

Don't ride all day. When in doubt, stop for some cake and think it through rather 55 than press on. Children are resilient, but they won't always thank you for dragging them 15 miles further. If you're cycling point-to-point, rather than from a fixed base, this may mean revising your travel plans. We halved our first-day's mileage after struggling on that long climb.

As it was, we retraced the High Peak Trail to Matlock where we took a cable car up to 60 the Heights of Abraham. At the top, the old lead mines have been turned into show caves. They've been show caves since Victorian times, when well-heeled ladies and gents were lowered down in baskets, sold quick-burning candles for a penny, then charged another penny to be rescued and hauled to the surface when their candles burned out. Today, electric lighting lines the route and the guides aren't so opportunistic. The Victorians 65 would have toured by train, of course; and it's thanks to their industry that we've now got such splendid tracks to cycle on. While you can cycle by road in the Peak District, you're best on the little wiggly yellow roads – with a light load. It's a bit hilly, you know.

Getting there: By road, Matlock is 20 minutes from the M1 (J28/29). Hartington is 9 miles from Buxton, where the 442 bus leaves for both Ashbourne and 70 Hartington. Matlock and Buxton are the closest railway stations, but if you want to take your own bikes you're restricted to two – and no tandems – on these services. A trailerbike counts as a bike. Matlock (change at Derby) is served by Central Trains (0121-6541200, www.centraltrains.co.uk). Reservations are free. Buxton (change at Manchester Piccadilly) is served by First North Western (0870 2412305, 75 www.firstnorthwestern.co.uk): bikes are free, but there are only two spaces allocated on a first-come, first-serve basis.

Where to stay: A dormitory bed in a Youth Hostel costs an average of £10 per adult or £6.90 for under-18s. Separate family rooms are available at larger hostels, costing around £40. To stay at a Youth Hostel you must be a member, which costs £25 per year 80 for a family. To join, call 0870 8708808, www.yha.org.uk.

The Guardian

Preparing for NCTs

Worksheet 106

Performance criteria for writing

Name:
Form:

This worksheet contains the performance criteria that examiners use to assess students' responses to the writing task in the NC English test, and to award a particular level to each response.
The performance criteria assess the students' ability to display the following six features in their writing:
- To communicate ideas to the reader;
- To use a style and tone that is appropriate for the chosen form of writing;
- To organize their writing appropriately;
- To develop and shape their writing using punctuation, paragraphs and grammatical structures;
- To use words precisely and appropriately and spell them correctly;
- To write neatly and legibly.

Performance criteria for level 4 (8–12 marks)
- The students' ideas are generally clear.
- They are beginning to use descriptive words effectively, although this may not be maintained throughout the piece.
- Their ideas are mostly organized in an appropriate form for a piece of personal writing.
- Some complex sentences have been used. Punctuation is mostly used accurately to mark sentences and students are beginning to use punctuation within sentences.
- Some interesting words have been selected and the spelling of simple and common polysyllabic words is generally accurate.
- Handwriting is mostly clear and legible.

Performance criteria for level 5 (14–18 marks)
- The students' writing is clearly expressed.
- They try to engage the reader's interest by such means as expression of feelings or description of setting or events.
- Their ideas are structured in an appropriate form for a piece of personal writing.
- Simple and complex sentences are usually organized into a clear structure or paragraphs. A range of punctuation, including commas and apostrophes, is usually used accurately.
- A reasonably wide vocabulary is used, though some words may not be used precisely. Spelling, including that of words with complex regular patterns, is usually accurate.
- Handwriting is generally clear and legible in a fluent style.

Performance criteria for level 6 (20–24 marks)
- The students' writing is interesting and engaging in parts.
- They use an appropriate style for a piece of personal writing describing events and feelings.
- Their ideas are structured in an appropriate form.
- A range of simple and complex sentences and appropriate paragraphing is used, though not necessarily throughout the piece. A range of punctuation is usually used correctly to clarify meaning.
- A varied vocabulary contributes to the effectiveness of the writing. Spelling is accurate though there may be some errors in difficult words.
- Handwriting is in a fluent and legible style.

Performance criteria for level 7 (26–30 marks)
- The students' writing is confident.
- They write in an appropriate and engaging style for a piece of personal writing.
- Their ideas are organized and written in an appropriate form.
- A range of grammatical features is used to build up the reader's interest. Paragraphing and correct punctuation are used to make the ideas clear.
- The effective use of vocabulary builds up the reader's interest. Spelling, including that of complex irregular words, is correct.
- Handwriting is in a fluent and legible style.

Preparing for NCTs

Assessing students' writing

Worksheet 107

Extract 1

Have you ever seen the dawn rise high above the clouds? Flying is like being a bird in the sky. Magic. Before making the journey I had complained about the early start and grumbled when I didn't have time to eat my breakfast, but all these resentments disappeared as I looked from my widow in the airplane and saw the distant golden glow of the sun gradually set fire to the clouds, engulfing us in its majestic and powerful glory. The grey airport town of Luton was left far behind, our distant destination of Glasgow wasn't even a glimer on the horizon. It was a journey that I didn't want to end - ever, even if it meant missing Granma's special birthday party.

Extract 2

Dawn. Magical time of day. First a soft cherry glow on the palid, puffy clouds below, gradually spreading paintbrush splashes, magenta, crimson, scarlet, ever changing before my eyes. A glorious sight that will remain with me always. This is my most memorable journey. Even without that glorious performance of the sky at dawn, it would have been special. My first flight. It might seem mundane and ordinary to others, but to me that journey from Luton to Glasgow to visit my Grandmother was exceptional. I had anticipated the early rise, the seeming hours of waiting, increasing tension and expectations, but seeing that dawn from my cramped seat, through the oval window, as the plane hung suspended in the air, was beyond my imaginings.

Extract 3

The best journey that I have ever made was on a plane from Luton to Glasgow. It was early in the morning so we had to rise before dawn and eat our breakfast only 1 piece of toast and catch the bus to the airport. As I live in St. Albans only 12 miles away, this was not to bad. The we had to check in and wait for our flight. This was boring and I was very tired and hungry but I put up with it because I knew it would be exciting once I was on the plane. My Mum and sister were with me, as we were going to visit my Gran because it was her seveteeth birthday. We were called to bord the plane and then I started to feel that something incredible was going to happen – I had never been on a plane before. Mum said I could sit by the window. I waited anxiously for the take-off.

Extract 4

Women pilots are few and far between, even these days, but I will always remeber that journey, my first flight, which inspired me to take up this very special career. Memories of youth, no doubt tinged with a rosy glow as the years have followed on, but vivid and clear nevertheless. My mother had a desire to celebrate the ocassion of Grandma's seventieth birthday and my father purchased tickets for us to fly from Luton to Glasgow. We must have risen early, because my most enduring memory of the journey was the exhillarrating experiance of seeing the sun rise high and golden red above the clouds. It was like being at the centre of the universe.

Preparing for NCTs

Worksheet 108

The writing question

Name
Form

Section C

This section of the paper is a test of writing. You will be assessed on:

- *your ideas and the way you organize and express them;*
- *your ability to write clearly, using paragraphs and accurate grammar, spelling and punctuation.*

Choose ONE of the following:

EITHER
a) Write a report for a magazine about a holiday you have enjoyed. Explain why parents should consider this to be a good choice for them and their family.

In your report you could:

- use a headline and subheadings where appropriate;
- give information about where you went, the time of year, duration of your stay, costs, etc;
- make comments about the activities and opportunities for families to enjoy themselves;
- describe accommodation and eating facilities;
- explain why this is a good choice for parents and children.

Write in paragraphs, but do not set your report out in columns. You may indicate where pictures, maps, etc. could be placed, but no credit will be given for artwork.

33 marks

OR
With global warming and ever-decreasing natural resources, people across the world are considering other forms of transport to replace the energy-unfriendly, polluting, petrol-driven motorcar.

b) Write a letter to your local Member of Parliament giving your views on the alternatives to cars as forms of transport, such as bicycles, trams, buses, trains.

In your letter you could:

- write in favour or against alternative types of transport;
- describe the problems created by too many cars on the road;
- explain your point of view;
- offer solutions to the transport problem as you see them;
- persuade the MP that your views should be taken into consideration.

Set your letter out in the conventional format, including addresses (which you may invent), date, greeting and ending.

33 marks

Preparing for NCTs

Worksheet 109

Shakespeare challenge: *Macbeth*

Name
Form

1 At the beginning of Act 2 scene 1 what do Macbeth and Banquo talk about?

✓ Bonus point: Who else was with Banquo at the start of the scene?

2 What does Macbeth mean towards the end of Act 2 scene 1 when he says, 'I go, and it is done; the bell invites me'?

✓ Bonus point: What are the last two lines of the scene that follow this quotation?

3 In Act 2 scene 2 what does Lady Macbeth reveal about herself when she gives her reason for not taking part in the killing of Duncan herself?

✓ Bonus point: In what type of speech does she make this revelation?

4 What is Macbeth's frame of mind when he returns from Duncan's chamber?

✓ Bonus point: Give one piece of evidence such as something he says or does that indicates his feelings.

5 How does Lady Macbeth try to cover up her husband's strange behaviour in Act 3 scene 4?

✓ Bonus point: In the end, when Macbeth does not seem to become any calmer, what does Lady Macbeth do?

6 What do Macbeth's final words, 'We are yet but young in deed', tell us about his state of mind at the end of Act 3 scene 4?

✓ Bonus point: How can this point in the play be described as a turning point in terms of Macbeth's character?

English Frameworking 3: Teacher's Resources   © HarperCollins Publishers 2002

Preparing for NCTs

Two Shakespeare questions

Worksheet 110

Name
Form

EITHER

Macbeth
Act 2 Scene 2

TASK 1

In this scene Macbeth returns to his wife following the murder of Duncan, and Lady Macbeth tries to ensure that all will be well.

Compare the response of Macbeth and Lady Macbeth to the murder of Duncan and comment on the dramatic impact that it creates.

Before you begin to write you should think about:

- the attitudes of Macbeth and Lady Macbeth concerning the murder;
- Macbeth's state of mind before and after his visit to Duncan's chamber;
- Lady Macbeth's response to her husband;
- the final part of the scene, including the knocking at the door.

Read the task again before you begin to write your answer.

OR

Macbeth
Act 3 Scene 4

TASK 2

In this scene Macbeth learns that Banquo has been killed. During the banquet that he is hosting for the thanes of Scotland, the ghost of Banquo haunts Macbeth, whose behaviour disturbs the guests who cannot see the vision.

Imagine that you are Macbeth. Write your thoughts and feelings concerning the events of the evening.

You could begin:
Why cannot Banquo lie still in his grave? Tonight I suffered and was tormented by his ghostly figure appearing before me.

Before you begin you should think about:
- the fact that Fleance is still alive;
- the appearance of Banquo's ghost and what it means;
- whether or not Macbeth really feels guilty for all that he has done;
- Macbeth's plans for the future.

Remember to write as if you are Macbeth.
Read the task again before you begin to write your answer.

Preparing for NCTs

Worksheet 111

Paper 2: Shakespeare play

Name
Form

Remember
- The test is 1 hour 15 minutes long.
- You should do **one** task on **one** play.
- Your work will be assessed for your knowledge and understanding of the play and the way you express your ideas.
- Check your work carefully.
- Ask your teacher if you are not sure what to do.

EITHER

Macbeth

Act 2 Scene 1 and Act 3 Scene 4

TASK 1

In these two scenes Macbeth sees firstly the vision of the dagger leading to Duncan's chamber and then the ghost of Banquo at the banquet.

How does Shakespeare use the element of the supernatural to develop the character of Macbeth in these two scenes?

Explain why this aspect of the play, in particular, would have engaged the interest of his audience at the time the play was written.

Before you begin to write you should think about these questions:
- What do these supernatural events tell us about Macbeth's state of mind and how do they affect his behaviour?
- What do we learn about Macbeth's character as a result of these visions?
- What does the use of the supernatural tell us about Shakespeare's ability to engage the interest of his audience?

Read the task again before you begin to write your answer.

OR

Macbeth

Act 2 Scene 2

TASK 2

In this scene Macbeth returns to his wife following the murder of Duncan.

Imagine that you have been asked to direct this scene for a class performance.

What advice would you give to your actors to create an atmosphere and make the scene interesting to the audience?

Before you begin to write you should decide:
- How you would interpret Lady Macbeth's response to her husband when he returns from Duncan's chamber;
- How you would want Macbeth to appear through the way he speaks his words;
- How you would make the scene interesting to the audience through the body language and actions of the characters on the stage.

Read the task again before you begin to write your answer.

Preparing for NCTs: Looking ahead to GCSEs

Worksheet 112

GCSE English

Name:
Form:

Your final GCSE English grade comes from three different types of assessment, which are usually made up as follows:

60% from the English examinations, Papers 1 and 2

The two examination papers are taken in June of Year 11.

Paper 1 tests your reading and writing skills in a media/non-fiction context, usually focusing on a particular issue. You will be asked to read and analyse the passage, then write a response. Some examination boards will give you pre-released material that allows you to prepare for the topic covered. The exam is usually about two hours long.

Paper 2 tests your literary reading and writing skills. The passage will come from a fiction text. Many exam boards release the actual text before the examination so that you can prepare properly and take the examination with a good understanding of the passage. The focus of the questions will often centre on the author's craft, or require an analysis of how an atmosphere, character or setting is created. This is followed by an opportunity for your own personal writing on various suggested topics, linked in some way with the given text. The examination is again about two hours long.

20% from a file of coursework

The **coursework file** consists of English and literature assignments, which you are required to complete during the two years of the course. The contents of the assignments are stipulated by the exam board. You will work on certain set pieces, which usually need to be a minimum of 400 words long, during English lessons and for homework. It will be up to you to spend your time thoughtfully planning and drafting your work with care, so that it shows you at your best.

Many students like coursework because it allows you to show what you can do when you have the time to think things through and make a thorough study of a topic or text. It does mean, however, that you can't leave everything to the last minute before your exams. You need to work hard throughout the two years in order to make sure that your coursework is completed to a high standard.

Note Different examination boards will have different approaches and requirements in terms of coursework and examinations. The outline given above is therefore a rough guide; your teacher will explain in more detail about the course that you will actually be taking.

20% from a speaking and listening assessment

The **speaking and listening assessment** is given by your teacher. Different examination boards have different approaches to the assessment of speaking and listening. But all have one thing in common – you will need to complete a variety of tasks, in different situations – some in groups, such as discussions, and some individual, such as giving a talk.

The exam boards may require you to complete formal set pieces for assessment or they may request an 'on going' assessment of your speaking and listening through the normal activities that you undertake in the classroom. Your teacher will explain the approaches that you will be using during your course.

Note Very strict guidelines are given about your conduct during these examinations. They are taken very seriously and anyone breaking the rules will have their GCSE results cancelled.

The papers are sent away to be marked by external examiners. The process of ensuring that they have been marked fairly takes a long time. Your results are sent to you in the last part of August.

Preparing for NCTs: Looking ahead to GCSEs

Worksheet 113

Reading self-evaluation sheet

Name
Form

1 Describe your attitude towards reading books on your own. For example, do you enjoy reading, do you put it off as a chore, or do you read occasionally when there is nothing else to do?

2 What type of books do you most enjoy reading on your own? You could name actual examples, or give a genre such as science fiction. Try to include both fiction and non-fiction.

3 What have you most enjoyed reading as part of your English course in Years 7 to 9? Think about novels, plays, poetry, autobiography …

4 Do you generally enjoy fiction more than non-fiction, or the other way around? Explain the reasons for your response.

5 What do you think has been the most challenging text you have ever read on your own or in class?

6 Do you enjoy reading magazines or comics in preference to books? If so, give your reasons, or explain why you prefer books.

7 When you read a novel, play or poem, what do you consider to be important factors in helping you decide whether you think it is good or not? Give each category (below) a score from 1 to 5, with 5 being very important and 1 being unimportant.

What makes a good read		Rating
A	The text needs to look inviting and presented in an interesting way, such as an unusual title or a bright cover.	
B	I need to be able to relate to the characters in a play or a novel, so that I can appreciate them and their point of view.	
C	The story line must catch my attention from the beginning or I will lose interest and not continue with it.	
D	I like to read about things that take me beyond my own experience, for example books set in other countries and cultures, fantasy or science fiction.	
E	The way something is written is important to me. There should be interesting vocabulary and imagery that helps me to imagine the setting and what is happening.	
F	I like books where there is a good balance between action, speech and description.	

- My greatest strength as a reader is that I _____

- In order to improve my reading I need to _____

Preparing for NCTs: Looking ahead to GCSEs — Worksheet 114

Reading: setting goals and challenges

pg 147

Name:
Form:

Complete the following statement.

I enjoy reading _____ (name a genre, author or title) and would like to read something similar such as _____ because I think it will be good.

As I normally prefer reading _____ I think it would be good to try something different, such as _____ (name a different type of genre or text).

Most of the books I have read were written before/after 1900 (delete as appropriate), therefore it would widen my experience to choose to read _____ (name a time period, or an author if you prefer).

If I wanted to read something that was different from or shorter than a novel I could try reading a _____ such as _____ for a change.

A real reading challenge for me would be to read _____ because _____

My reading goals are to:

1 _____
2 _____
3 _____

Reading is an important part of my future because _____

Preparing for NCTs: Looking ahead to GCSEs — Worksheet 115

What makes a useful target?

Name:
Form:

Remember that targets should be SMART:

> **S** pecific – clearly defined and understood.
> **M** easurable – so that you know if and when the target has been hit.
> **A** chievable – not slt, which is discouraging; not too easy, which is a waste of time.
> **R** elevant – to the specific task and audience.
> **T** ime limited – there must be a deadline.

The targets below were set by a Year 9 student as part of a literacy course. How good are they as targets? Work in groups to grade the targets, using the following system:

> Ex = excellent – covers all or most of the requirements of a SMART target;
> OK = okay – covers some of the requirements of a SMART target;
> X = useless – covers hardly any of the requirements of a SMART target.

1. Settle down to work quickly and display appropriate behaviour.

2. Read a range of newspapers and at least one book a week next term, including at least two books outside my normal reading programme.

3. Ask my teacher for help when I don't understand anything.

4. Record at least 10 spelling corrections in my spelling log per week and learn them using the appropriate strategies.

5. Improve my writing, reading and spelling by the end of the year.

6. Read at least two newspapers every day.

7. Improve the quality of my written presentation.

8. Improve my ability to link ideas effectively in the paragraphs that I write next half term.

9. Speak coherently, using only brief notes, when making formal presentations next term.

10. Be more confident when speaking in class.

Preparing for NCTs: Looking ahead to GCSEs

Worksheet 116

Reviewing your reading skills

Name:
Form:

As a reader, what do you do well? Give yourself a score for each of the statements below, with 5 being the highest (excellent) and 1 being the lowest (needs improving).

Reading skills	Score
A I can read a wide range of different types of texts – media, fiction and non-fiction	
B I am able to skim and scan texts quickly to form a general impression and select information	
C I can find and extract useful information without simply copying when doing research	
D I understand the purpose of a text, for example whether it is persuasive or giving advice	
E I can analyse an author's tone and style and I am able to discuss the effect that the writing creates for the reader	
F I know about the English literary heritage and have read some texts that were written before 1900	
G I enjoy reading fiction on my own for pleasure	
H I enjoy reading non-fiction for pleasure as well as for information	
I I read newspapers and magazines regularly	
J I learn from what I read and use the knowledge, skills and information that it gives me to my advantage	

Set yourself two targets for improvement:

● ....

● ....

English Frameworking 3: Teacher's Resources   © HarperCollins Publishers 2002

Preparing for NCTs: Looking ahead to GCSEs

Worksheet 117

Reviewing your writing skills (pg 149)

Name:
Form:

As a writer, what do you do well? Give yourself a score for each of the statements below, with 5 being the highest (excellent) and 1 being the lowest (needs improving).

Writing skills	Score
A I can write in a way that takes account of my audience so that I vary my style and vocabulary to suit their needs	
B I can write in different forms, such as letters, leaflets and essays, and for a range of different purposes	
C I can develop my ideas in organized paragraphs	
D I can vary the length and construction of my sentences to create different effects	
E My descriptive writing, and use of imagery, is interesting and effective in creating an appropriate atmosphere	
F I can present and argue a case to influence or persuade my readers	
G I can write a balanced analysis that considers various aspects of a question	
H I take care with my spelling and check words using a dictionary or spell-checker when I am unsure	
I I can draft my work, listen to advice about how to make improvements and act on what is said	
J I can use a range of presentational devices where they are appropriate, such as bullet points, italics, underlining, etc.	

Set yourself two targets for improvement:

- ....
  ....

- ....
  ....